# The Railway Paintings of
# Barry J. Freeman

**MIDLAND TRAILS**
30in x 24in

# THE RAILWAY PAINTINGS OF
# BARRY J. FREEMAN

**Barry J. Freeman** BA GRA FRSA

Silver Link Publishing Ltd

First published in 2008

British Library Cataloguing in Publication Data

A catalogue record for this book is available from the British Library.

ISBN 978 1 85794 314 6

Silver Link Publishing Ltd
The Trundle
Ringstead Road
Great Addington
Kettering
Northants NN14 4BW

Tel/Fax: 01536 330588
email: sales@nostalgiacollection.com
Website: www.nostalgiacollection.com

Printed and bound in the Czech Republic

# BARRY JOHN FREEMAN

**BA GRA FRSA** was born in Northampton in 1937. He was educated at Northampton Grammar School and later, as a mature student, at the City of Leicester College of Education, where he qualified as a teacher.

He served for ten years in the Royal Navy, followed by several years in the electronics and aviation industries before becoming a teacher in 1971. He taught drawing and painting for 18 years until early retirement provided the opportunity to become a professional artist in 1989.

An avid railway enthusiast since childhood, his combined love of art and railways is reflected in the highly detailed paintings in which he now specialises. He works almost exclusively in oils and, on average, a painting takes at least two months to complete. His insistence on accuracy means that a similar amount of time is spent on research in the extensive library of books and photographs he has built up over the years.

He is a full member of the Guild of Railway Artists and is a former Deputy President of the Guild. His paintings have been reproduced in many forms, including collectors' plates, book covers, postcards, greetings cards, jigsaw puzzles and calendars, as well as fine art prints, which can now be found in many parts of the world. He has featured in numerous railway publications and has written several articles on painting for *The Artist* and *Artists' and Illustrators'* magazines.

His hobbies include classical music and travel; he and his wife Mary, who is also his business manager, have to date visited just over 100 countries worldwide.

He has featured on BBC radio and both Anglia and Central Television in connection with his work. He was elected a Fellow of the Royal Society of Arts in 1995.

*Title page* Barry Freeman in the cab of No 70000 *Britannia* at Didcot.

*Right* Working on 'Light Duties'.

# INTRODUCTION

My first recollection of travelling by train dates from 1946, at the beginning of a holiday to North Wales from my home in Northampton. I remember as though it were yesterday the excitement at the prospect of a train journey, the train steaming into Platform 7 at Castle station and my father saying, 'Look here, we have a named engine.' It was a 'Royal Scot', No 6156 *The South Wales Borderer*. The journey took in the wonders of such hives of activity as Rugby, Crewe and Chester, and by the time we arrived at Penmaenmawr, on the North Wales coast, I was hooked. Looking back, some 60-odd years later, I suppose that this early memory was the beginning of a lifetime's interest, or indeed passion. Little did I think that 40 years later I would have the chance to make a career of painting railways, but this is how it has been for the past 20 years now.

Having returned from that first holiday after the end of the Second World War, I couldn't wait to see and find out more about this wonderful world of railways. Ian Allan *ABC* books, listing the locomotives belonging to the four companies existing at the time, were becoming available and it soon became evident that there was a whole new world out there waiting to be discovered. In company with a group of school friends, I began to investigate the possibilities of venturing further afield to see what other treasures were to be found. Bike rides to Roade and Blisworth and train rides to Rugby and Bletchley soon followed, and it wasn't long before my friends and I became curious as to what we might see outside our LMS environment.

I have always counted myself fortunate in being born in Northampton, as no fewer than five main railway lines crossed the county. The East Coast Main Line passed through Peterborough, which was then in Northamptonshire; the LMS main lines from both Euston and St Pancras and the old Great Central passed through the centre; and the Great Western from Paddington to Birmingham and the north passed through Aynho and King's Sutton, in the far south-west of the county. We soon discovered that United Counties buses would, for a shilling or two, take us to such places as Wellingborough, Kettering and Peterborough, all of which would produce a stream of locomotives never seen at Northampton. Peterborough was a Mecca for LNER 'Pacifics'. The Midland main line was heavily populated by 'Jubilees',

'Compounds' and, on occasion, the weird and wonderful Beyer-Garratts. The old Great Central line delivered another selection of LNER 'A3' 'Pacifics', including, on occasion, *Flying Scotsman* itself. Only the Great Western was at this time (1947) a closed book to us, until we found a train that would take us to Banbury. This, to a group of 10-and-11-year-olds, was almost the other side of the world and involved a journey of some 30 miles on the erstwhile Stratford upon Avon & Midland Junction Railway from Blisworth to Banbury Merton Street. The first time we took this trip, we rushed from Merton Street to the main station, Banbury General, to be greeted 3 minutes after arrival by the sight of a down express hauled by a vision in green, with shining copper and brass and the biggest nameplate we had ever seen. The engine was 'Star' Class No 4061 *Glastonbury Abbey*. I couldn't take my eyes off it and from that moment became a lifelong fan of anything Great Western.

In 1948 I began secondary education at Northampton Grammar School, which, among many other extra-curricular activities, had a railway club. Several of my friends also won scholarships, so we continued our spotting trips almost as though nothing had happened. The railway club was run by one of the science masters, who was even more of a railway fanatic than any of us. It was during a visit to Bletchley in 1950 that we got the 'catch' of all time. He managed to persuade the shed foreman to let us visit the engine shed, where we found a Scottish 'Jubilee', No 45583 *Assam*. It was not in steam and had apparently failed, but none of us could understand why it was there, as engines from Corkerhill, Glasgow, were unheard of in our area. During all my subsequent railway trips over many years, including several tours of Scotland, I never saw it again.

It was around 1951 that my friends and I were introduced to the Railway Correspondence & Travel Society. This organisation had a branch in Northampton and ran monthly coach trips to numerous engine sheds across the country, always on Sundays. Over the succeeding four years, Bob, our regular driver, took us to most of the best-known sheds in Britain, not to mention some of the most obscure. He seemed to know the way to any shed, no matter how remote, although he had no particular interest in railways on his own account. In recent years numerous books have been published on the railways of Northamptonshire and the surrounding counties, and most of the photographs in them are by names I recognise from our RCTS days.

The early 1950s was also the era of the day excursion. It seemed that British Railways would put on an excursion to almost anywhere, seemingly at the drop of a hat. Our little group took advantage of numerous football specials, very peaceful affairs then, ending up in places such as Norwich, Bristol, Birmingham, Derby, Blackpool, London, Leeds, Manchester, Liverpool and many other parts of England. We never saw any of the football matches, but would spend the days happily spotting on the main stations. There were also many other excursions, some to the most unlikely places and for no apparent reason. We weren't concerned with the whys and wherefores, however, only the fact that they provided us with somewhere new to see on a regular basis.

It was at the Grammar School that I met my first real art teacher, the formidable David Gommon. He was what we thought of as a 'proper painter' and, in an oblique way, fired my enthusiasm for the subject as a whole. Looking back, what he did, in a very unobtrusive way, was to introduce us to all the basics of being an artist. He made us look and think differently, although many of us did not realise it at the time. I had always considered myself fairly good at the subject, but Mr Gommon had any amount of subtle ways of demonstrating that perhaps you weren't as good as you thought you were. He would arrive very quietly and stand looking over your shoulder, sometimes for as much as 10 minutes, without saying anything at all. Then, just when you thought you might have achieved something a little special, the standard comment would be almost whispered, 'Hmm, not very good is it?' He would then spend the next 10 minutes or so suggesting minor adjustments, all of which made sense when a little thought was applied. Six years of this, I am certain, went a long way towards making me the artist I am today.

I would have loved to have carried on my artistic activities after I left school, but National Service was rearing its ugly head and although I was successful in an interview to be a quantity surveyor, the company was unable to commit themselves to holding a post open for a new recruit for two whole years. It was while I was looking around for something to do for the period between

Members of the Northampton Grammar School railway club outside Castle station before a visit to Bletchley in June 1950 – I am second from the left. Note the excursion advertised on the station wall: Blisworth Hotel swimming pool for 1 shilling! The regular engine on the Blisworth trains at the time was a lovely old LNWR Webb 2-4-2 passenger tank, No 46666.

leaving school and being called for National Service that one of my friends told me he was going to work for British Railways, having been tempted by talk of privilege tickets and free passes. This sounded good to me so I also applied and soon found myself a very small cog in a very large wheel at Rugby Midland station. The privilege tickets and free passes were indeed available, and during the next year and a half we used them to visit almost every area of Britain.

However, National Service was drawing ever closer and, having found out the rates of pay, I decided that existing on the princely sum of 7 shillings a day was bordering on the impossible. I therefore decided to join the services as a regular. My railway interests had a strong influence in my choice of service. I had for years been fascinated by some of the exotic names associated with the then British Empire as allocated to the LMS ' Jubilees', so I joined the Royal Navy, thinking that I might be lucky enough to actually see some of them. During the following 10 years I did see quite a few foreign countries, became involved in a couple of minor wars and, among other things, played a lot of cricket.

During this time, art took very much a back seat and it was not until some years later that I got the chance to re-acquaint myself with the subject. I had spent a couple of years in the electronics and aviation industries after leaving the Navy when the opportunity came to train as a teacher. I applied and was successful, eventually qualifying with art as a main subject. Being a mature student after having been in charge of a large number of people in the Navy was a somewhat strange experience, particularly as some of the tutors were younger than I was. I found a post in a medium-sized comprehensive school in Northamptonshire, where for the next 18 years I tried to put into practice all I had learned so many years before, eventually evolving my own methods of turning pupils into artists and for much of that time thinking I had one of the best jobs in the world.

This career might well have continued until retirement, but in November 1988 things were to change in the most drastic and unforeseen way imaginable. Shortly before this, my wife Mary had been given, and accepted, the opportunity of taking early retirement. Over a weekend I was stricken by a virus, the effects of which took 18 months to finally disappear. I was unable to return to teaching after such a long absence and was offered early retirement as well, so we found ourselves, almost at a stroke, with no careers and no salaries. It was obvious that we needed to take a new direction in life, so we set to thinking about what we could do with our various qualifications. Mary had only recently completed a postgraduate Diploma in Management Studies, achieving a Distinction. I knew quite a bit about ships and aircraft in addition to railways, having spent almost all my time in the Navy with the Fleet Air Arm. We realised that we had a ready-made and probably unique partnership right from the start, so the decision was fairly easy. We would set up a small business. She became my business manager and dealt with the many and varied demands that setting up and running a small business entailed. I became a transport artist and, in effect, the workforce. Our new partnership gave me the opportunity to concentrate entirely on painting and I have ever since been grateful that, unlike most artists, I was spared the unenviable task of having to 'sell myself'. In the event, I very soon became 'typecast' as a railway artist and the majority of my work over the years has been in this field, other forms of transport taking very much a secondary role.

Almost from the start, and largely due to Mary's persistence, we began to have some success. We put four paintings into print and toured preservation societies and model railway exhibitions all over the country selling them. In time we added to our repertoire with more prints, followed by postcards, greetings cards, collectors' plates, jigsaw puzzles, book covers and so on. After two or three years we found that we didn't have to push so hard and people began to contact us rather than the other way around, having seen my work displayed in its various forms around the country. During this time we both worked for anything up to 18 hours a day, either painting, selling, driving a car full of prints around the country to locations as far apart as Carnforth and Cornwall, or exhibiting at preservation societies, model railway shows and museums. Commissions began to materialise and for much of the past 20 years this has been the pattern of our existence.

Railway enthusiasts can be very exacting and extremely knowledgeable about their subject. For every painting, total accuracy and complete authenticity are therefore essential. Part of the research for each painting includes a location visit, which helps me to absorb at least some of the atmosphere, although much of the network that existed during the steam age has now disappeared and many of the remaining locations have radically changed. Consequently, much of my work consists of painstaking reconstructions of specific pieces of railway

history, with the result that I often find myself being almost as much a historian as an artist.

I now work almost exclusively in oils, using Winsor & Newton artists' colours. I also use their 'Liquin' medium extensively for its quick-drying properties. In addition, its use is invaluable in allowing me to produce the fine detail my clients demand. Over the years I have reduced what started out as a large collection of brushes to a comparatively few favourites. For broader work I use long-bristled flat brushes in various sizes, while more detailed work such as fine detailing and highlighting is done using a variety of sable riggers and watercolour brushes. These do not take too kindly to working on canvas and I often have to buy several new ones for each painting. The old ones are used for blending small areas of colour, with a number of sable fan blenders for larger areas such as sky and smoke effects. My canvases come from Messrs Bird & Davis in London and are exclusively their No 13 Belgian Linen. This has a very fine 'tooth', which allows the finest detail to be produced fairly easily.

I start each painting with a pencil drawing direct on to the canvas. This is reinforced with a fine rigger and a thin mix of black. When this has dried, the whole canvas receives a thin coat of burnt umber. This gives it a mid-tone, which I find much easier to work with than blank white. I then decide on the direction of the lighting, the time of day, the time of year, the direction of the railway at the particular location and the weather

Portrait of the artist: working on 'Bright Intervals' and 'Light Duties'.

conditions. When completed, the painting should be 'readable', that is to say that it should be possible to gauge such factors as the direction of the wind, whether the engine is working hard or coasting and so on.

I have often been asked how I know when a painting is finished. Resisting the temptation to say 'When someone comes and takes it away', the answer has to be that it is very difficult to decide. My method is as follows. When the painting is in its last stages, I make a list of everything still to be included. When all the items are crossed off the list, the painting is complete.

Much of my work has involved re-creating the personal memories of my clients. The only problem with this is that memories over a long period tend to become compressed into a single one. On several occasions I have been requested to include features in a painting that could not possibly have existed at the time the painting was to be set. This has, on occasion, resulted in a little judicious 'arm-twisting' in order to keep things accurate. Changes in the liveries of locomotives and rolling stock also have to be carefully researched, not to mention numerous differences in detail between members of the same class. For example, the LMS 'Princess Royals', in a class of only 12 engines, had three different patterns of valve gear. Research can often be something of a minefield, but it can be quite fascinating sorting out all the different details for a painting, so much so that the research often takes longer than the painting itself.

One evening, while driving home from my parents' home in Somerset, we happened to pass over the bridge at the end of Lower Heyford station, on the Oxford to Banbury line. It looked a perfect location for a painting, with the canal running close alongside the railway and the village as a backdrop. My wife suggested that we should include canals as well as railways in the paintings. She had noticed that at exhibitions the wives had a considerable input into whether a print was purchased and were more likely to accept a picture featuring boats as well as trains. This opened up a whole new area of research, plus a sizeable extension to my library, and has been a feature of my work, whenever I could find suitable locations, ever since.

Looking back over what is now quite a long and, in some ways, a very varied life, I realise that I wouldn't have missed a moment of it. Thanks are due to innumerable people along the way, but in particular to my wife Mary. The last 20 years have been very much a team effort and I am quite certain that without her expertise and support a great deal of what has been achieved, including this book, would never have happened. I hope that you will enjoy looking at the pictures as much as I have enjoyed painting them.

# 'A DATE WITH THE "DUCHY"'

Anyone who has ever been on holiday to South Devon and Cornwall by rail will be familiar with the stretch of line between Starcross and Teignmouth, where the railway runs along the sea wall through Dawlish. Numerous classic locations exist in this area, and thousands of photographers and more than a few artists have portrayed the railway scene here. To my mind, the best location of all is at milepost 207, between the Parson's and Clerk's tunnels, just to the south-west of Dawlish. The spot affords a superb view of the characteristic red cliffs, with the beaches on the seaward side stretching away to Dawlish in the distance.

Arriving at the location involves a fairly long walk from the main road between Dawlish and Teignmouth. A footpath leads from near the Smugglers Inn across the fields to the coastal footpath, then down a steep hill to the spot between the two tunnels overlooking Shell Cove. Today, the location is very overgrown and one or two boulders have disappeared from the top of Horse Rocks, but not much else has changed in the general scene.

This is one of those scenes I had wanted to paint for many years so, when the opportunity arose, Mary and I set out to take location photographs. We spent several hours at the spot, taking numerous photographs with a 250mm lens of all the features I thought I might need for the painting. These were stuck together into a sort of collage, which was then used to re-create the scene. For the main subject, I chose the 1.30pm from Paddington to Penzance, which in 1955 acquired the title of 'The Royal Duchy'. This train was due into Newton Abbot just before 5.30 in the afternoon, a time that provided good shadows on the surrounding landscape. 'The Royal Duchy' was almost always worked by a 'Castle' Class 4-6-0, and for this painting I chose one of the later examples, No 7036 *Taunton Castle*.

The Western Region had something of a field day between 1955 and 1957 in creating named trains. Opinion at the time was that this was an excuse for painting sets of coaches in the old GWR chocolate and cream colours. Whatever the reason, the GWR colours look much better in a painting than anything else. The first chocolate and cream coaches appeared in June 1956, so I chose to set the picture in 1957, when many of the main-line sets had been re-painted. 'The Royal Duchy' headboard carried the arms of the Duchy of Cornwall and required the consent of HM the Queen for it to be displayed in this context.

The figures in the painting are two friends who actually live in Scotland. I needed to make a feature of the bank on the left of the picture so, while on a visit, they were co-opted to be the models for a couple who have stopped for a little light refreshment, perhaps while walking their dogs along the coastal path. A neighbour of ours has a lovely little Sheltie called Holly, who I thought would be perfect for the picture, so I gave her some temporary new owners and she now appears in the painting twice.

Shell Cove and Horse Rocks, Dawlish: this view, at milepost 207, was used for 'A Date with the "Duchy"'.

'A Date with the "Duchy"'
30in x 20in

# 'AN AUDIENCE WITH *KING EDWARD II'*

In my opinion, the fitting of double chimneys to Charles Collett's 'King' Class 4-6-0s ruined their looks, so I have never painted a 'King' with a double chimney (or a 'Castle' so fitted, come to that). It came as a very pleasant surprise to find that the Great Western Society had acquired No 6023 *King Edward II* with the intention of restoring it as close to its original appearance as possible. Various details had been added or altered after nationalisation, some of which it wasn't going to be possible to return to their original state, but it was good to have the chance to paint the preserved version much as I remembered them before they were disfigured.

While searching through my reference books for a suitable location, I came across a couple of photographs taken in the mid-1950s in Sydney Gardens, Bath, where the railway passes alongside a park with only a low wall separating the tracks from the park itself. This seemed perfect, so I set out on a location visit, wondering how the scene might have changed in the 40 years since the photographs were taken. On arriving in Sydney Gardens I found, to my amazement, that the scene had hardly changed at all. True, some of the trees had grown somewhat taller, but everything else appeared exactly the same. Even the smoke marks were still on the walls! This was a real bonus as I usually spend at least a couple of months trying to piece together a scene before the painting actually begins.

At the time the painting was started, the intention at Didcot was to put the engine into the Great Western 1947 livery, with the large 'G crest W' on the tender. At the time of writing, the restoration of the engine is almost complete and I understand that it will now appear in BR blue, probably the most unpopular livery applied to any engine due to its poor wearing qualities in traffic. Hopefully it will reappear in proper Great Western livery not too far into the future.

While the painting was in its early stages, we were visited by a friend, at the time an RAF Squadron Leader. He arrived in uniform and was immediately co-opted to model for two of the figures, although for the purposes of the painting we demoted him to Flight Lieutenant. My wife Mary became the schoolgirl, who is far more interested in the RAF officer than the train, and a couple of young spotters were added for good measure. Several years later, we were engaged in conversation by a lady who was visiting one of our exhibitions. She had been at school in Bath and was very keen to know how we knew the exact details of her old school uniform. We didn't like to tell her it was a total guess!

Sydney Gardens, Bath, one of the very rare locations
that has hardly changed at all in 50 years.

'An Audience with *King Edward II*'
36in x 24in

# 'BACK TO THE FUTURE'

Several years ago now, a friend who at the time was heavily involved with the group building the new Peppercorn 'A1' Class 'Pacific' at Darlington, asked me to paint him a picture showing how the locomotive might appear when complete and in service. This was the first time I'd been asked to 'look the other way', so to speak, as most of my work involves historical reconstructions. *Tornado* was very much in the early stages of construction, but I was assured that it would appear as a standard 'A1'. The number was to be 60163, but no livery had by then been decided. Although most of the class had first appeared in LNER green, 13, including the last 10, had entered service in British Railways blue, which soon acquired a reputation for not wearing well in service. The blue livery lasted only three years before being replaced by the more familiar Brunswick green, which remained their standard livery until the end of steam. Although the blue livery would probably have been more correct, we decided that Brunswick green was a better bet, as the 'A1s' spent most of their short lives in this livery.

Next, we had to decide where to set the painting. Apart from eastern Scotland, the only line we could think of where 'A1s' had worked and which wasn't half obscured by electric catenaries was the Settle & Carlisle line. We arranged to meet one morning at Penrith and from there we toured the whole length of the line looking for a suitable location. We had decided not to do the obvious (Ais Gill Viaduct) and to try and include scenery characteristic of the line. We eventually settled on Birkett Common, on the southbound climb to the summit at

Ais Gill. Given a westerly wind, this would keep the exhaust well out of the way and an elevated viewpoint would ensure an uninterrupted view of the train and the glorious background scenery across the Eden Valley.

Everything having been finally decided, I began the painting using the location photographs we had taken earlier. All went well until I realised that the engine's nameplates hadn't been fitted and I didn't know exactly where to paint the one that would appear in the picture. Three of the original class had been named after constituent companies of the LNER and included the company coat of arms above the name. The nameplates for *Tornado* were configured in much the same way, but a close study of the 'A1s' revealed that nameplates were fitted in a variety of positions, seemingly governed by the length of the name and, in the case of those with company coats of arms, the necessity to avoid the handrails on the smoke deflectors. A flurry of telephone calls between me, my friend and the then chief engineer ensued, culminating in the instruction, 'You paint it where you think it ought to be, and that's where we'll fit it!'

So, the completed painting shows *Tornado* with a southbound excursion, making a maximum effort on the last stages of the climb to Ais Gill. All our guesswork regarding liveries may have been to no avail, however. *Tornado* is now almost complete and recent reports state that it will probably appear, incorrectly, in LNER green. Perhaps one day it might receive a re-paint and appear as it does in the picture, which is now about eight years old.

'BACK TO THE FUTURE'
36in x 24in

# 'BRIGHT INTERVALS'

This painting involved another major reconstruction job. The location is Leamington Spa, which once possessed two stations side by side. The GWR station, Leamington Spa General, hasn't really changed very much over the years, but the LNWR station, Leamington Spa Avenue, which forms the background, has been totally demolished.

I had been asked to portray one of the final series of Charles Collett's 'Castle' Class locomotives, No 7027 *Thornbury Castle*, at Leamington for the locomotive's owner. He had 'discovered' the GWR at Leamington many years earlier on a spotting trip from his home in Coventry and wanted his engine, which at the time was a set of parts, put together in a painting.

Being more or less permanently in the shade of its larger GWR counterpart across the way, Leamington Spa Avenue produced very little by way of photographic references. It had some substantial station

buildings and a large footbridge, details of which were essential in order to complete the painting. In the end, Dick Blenkinsop, a very well-known railway photographer, came to the rescue with something over 30 of his own photographs taken from the down platform of the General station. A close study of these enabled me to piece together all the details of Avenue station, together with the beautifully complex signal post that stood on the northern end of the up platform at General.

My client was also closely concerned with the restoration of an LNWR 'Super D', No 49395, which at the time was also a set of parts in the National Railway Museum. It seemed a good opportunity to include this engine in the painting as well. A little artistic licence was necessary as, at the time the painting is set, it was allocated to Buxton and would have been a very unlikely visitor to Leamington. I decided to paint it in ex-works condition as though it had just emerged from repairs at Crewe and was running in before returning to its home shed.

For the main subject I chose to put *Thornbury Castle* on the 'Cambrian Coast Express', which did not stop at Leamington during the mid-1950s when the painting is set. This allowed a wider-angle view of the 'Castle' as it passes on the centre road and hopefully portrays the feeling of space that always existed at GWR stations that had originally been laid to broad gauge dimensions.

In the summer of 1956 the Western Region began to repaint sets of coaches in the old chocolate and cream colours for some of its named expresses, starting with the 'Torbay Express' and the 'Cornish Riviera'. Others, including the 'Cambrian Coast Express', were soon added, restoring the Great Western image that gave the Western Region of British Railways its unique flavour.

'Bright Intervals'
36in x 24in

# 'CASTLE COUNTRY'

The line from Paignton to Kingswear was unusual in that it was able to take the heaviest express engines, so it was quite common to find Great Western 'Kings', 'Castles' and 'Stars' on the single-track branch. I discovered this location during a period in Plymouth in the latter stages of my service in the Royal Navy. By now I had a car and spent many of my off-duty hours exploring the railways in Devon and Cornwall. The road from Paignton to Brixham crosses the line just to the west of Churston station, giving a lovely view of the rolling Devon countryside towards the Dart estuary and the small country station.

Following closure by British Railways in the early 1970s, the branch was taken over in 1972 as the Paignton & Dartmouth Steam Railway and is now a major tourist attraction in the South West of England. Churston station buildings and the station footbridge are much as they always were, but the area surrounding the station has now undergone extensive redevelopment and is hardly recognisable from the view in this painting.

I had been asked by a client living in Cornwall for a painting featuring the 'Torbay Express' at Churston. He asked specifically for the coaches to appear in the chocolate and cream livery and for the large headboard to be featured, but this gave rise to a real problem. It was in June 1956 that four sets of coaches were repainted in Great Western colours, two for the 'Cornish Riviera Express' and two for the 'Torbay Express'. At around this time a large building project began to appear in the fields immediately adjacent to the station. This was to be the new Churston Grammar School, which, when completed, masked most of the countryside to the right of this view. This put the whole painting in jeopardy and, being unable to find out for certain by other means whether the view was authentic, I visited the school during one of my location visits to find out exactly when it was built and opened. Having a perfect stranger walk through the main door and demand to know when the school was opened must have made the reception staff wonder what on earth was going on. They were very co-operative, however, and managed to find a member of staff who had been at the school since its opening. It transpired that the school was completed late in 1957 and that there was a short period during the early summer of 1956 when the building works did not intrude on the view from the Brixham road bridge. This is the view that now appears in the painting.

Since my early spotting trips to Banbury and Oxford, I had always admired the Great Western 'Castles'. They seemed to me to be some of the best-looking engines to be found anywhere in Britain. For this painting, I decided to portray No 5011 *Tintagel Castle*, which at the time was a Newton Abbot engine and one of the most likely to be found on the 'Torbay Express'. It is shown re-starting the express after its brief stop at Churston. In the bay to the left of the picture, Collett '1400' Class 0-4-2T No 1470, in charge of the Brixham branch auto-coach, waits for its next trip down the 2-mile branch to the coast.

'CASTLE COUNTRY'
30in x 20in

# 'CROSSING AT CORFE'

On one of our visits to the Swanage Railway, my wife and I met the owner of a nameplate that had once belonged to 'West Country' Class 'Pacific' No 34098 *Templecombe*. He was a volunteer on the line and, having seen some of my work, asked me if I would paint 'his' engine somewhere on the Swanage branch. Corfe Castle station seemed a natural choice, with its ruined castle as an impressive backdrop. *Templecombe* was a Bournemouth engine during the period after its rebuilding in February 1961 and would probably have been a regular performer on the expresses from Swanage to London. A visit to the location suggested that the view from the northern end of the down platform would offer the best possibilities, so location photographs were taken and everything seemed, at this point, to be plain sailing. Later in the day, back at Swanage station, I mentioned to one of the railway's directors that I would be painting a picture located on the branch. This immediately resulted in a request that I investigate the possibility of including No 34072 *257 Squadron* as well. This was an unrebuilt 'Battle of Britain' Class engine that had recently been restored at Swanage. My client was happy to have the painting adapted to include two trains, so on the way home we stopped off at Corfe again and took some more location photographs, which I hoped would include all the details I would need to complete the painting.

Both engines proved to be a problem, mainly with regard to their tenders – something of a minefield, as there are numerous variations. *257 Squadron*, as preserved, had one of the original unmodified high-sided tenders. I couldn't sort out which tender *Templecombe* had in 1961, so I enlisted the help of Mike Arscott, of the Bulleid Preservation Society, who confirmed that *Templecombe* was one of the few that retained its cut-down 4,500-gallon tender after rebuilding. *257 Squadron* was one of only four or five that still retained their original high-sided tenders.

Assembling all the details for the painting had its amusing side. Some of my location photographs showed the remains of a small structure just off the end of the down platform. I had no idea what it might have been and a search of my library produced absolutely nothing, so I contacted Colin Caddy and John Scrace, two well-known photographers who I knew had taken numerous shots at Corfe. Colin Caddy couldn't help, but John Scrace rang back to say that although he didn't have anything, his mother had. It turned out that she had been intending to take a photograph of the castle from the down platform, and had missed! The result was a perfect colour print of a small oil store, which had later been demolished, right down to the piece of wood that served as a makeshift door latch and the rust marks made by some nails that had been knocked into the door from the inside. It also showed the road alongside the station, which is now obscured by some tall trees.

All I needed now was a rebuilt 'West Country' at the right angle. Only one, *Taw Valley*, was operational at the time, and I managed to catch up with it at Folkestone Harbour, where it was running trains up the steep incline to the main line. I spent a very pleasant day watching all the activity in and around the harbour and managed to take all the photographs I needed. *Taw Valley* had quite a few non-standard features, particularly the tender, so in the painting I had to carry out some fairly extensive modifications. This turned out to be fairly easy once I knew exactly what a 4,500-gallon tender looked like.

The Swanage branch runs roughly south-east to north-west, so the only time of day when the light falls on the right-hand side of a northbound train is very early morning around mid-summer. The request to include *257 Squadron* as well as *Templecombe* created a very unusual set of circumstances, with two 'Pacifics' on the branch at the same time. *257 Squadron* was actually an Exmouth Junction engine at the time the painting is set (summer 1961), so I decided to make the second train an inter-regional excursion, which might have arrived at some time other than its timetable intended, the engine having been 'borrowed', perhaps from Salisbury, to work the last stages of the train's journey to Swanage.

'CROSSING AT CORFE'
36in x 24in

# 'DAYS OF RED AND GOLD'

As a very young spotter, I only ever saw one streamlined 'Coronation'. This was No 46243 *City of Lancaster*, the last one to lose its streamlined casing and the only streamlined example to have carried its British Railways number following nationalisation in January 1948. It was only in later years that I realised how lucky I'd been, although at the time it meant very little. The engine was in unlined black and looked thoroughly dishevelled under a coating of grime and with the number only just visible. Nevertheless, it was a streamlined 'Coronation' and, looking back after almost 60 years, I wish I'd taken more notice or, even better, had a camera!

This painting shows another of the class, No 6239 *City of Chester*, and was commissioned by the owner of one of the locomotive's nameplates. The only brief was that the locomotive should be shown in its original streamlined form. The location was left to me, so I chose what is, in my opinion, the most spectacular scenery to be found anywhere on the West Coast route, the Lune Gorge, north of Lancaster. I always thought it rather odd that this line acquired the title of the 'West Coast' route, as for almost all of the 401 miles between London and Glasgow it is nowhere near the coast; only on the short stretch skirting Morecambe Bay is there a fleeting view of the sea.

Shortly after passing Oxenholme on its way north, the line swings inland to negotiate the deep valley through the hills created by the River Lune. I decided on a northbound train on the basis that the surrounding scenery gave a better composition to the picture, and settled on a spot close to the site of Dillicar water troughs. The location visit proved interesting as the place I'd chosen proved to be on the southbound carriageway of the M6!

*City of Chester* was perhaps one of the less well-known members of the class. It was built out of sequence, ahead of No 6238, and entered traffic at the end of August 1939. I decided to set the painting in the autumn of 1939, soon after the engine was built and while it still retained some of its original splendour. I couldn't find a photograph of a streamlined 'Duchess' at the right angle anywhere in my collection, so I reconstructed one from a de-streamlined example. Only having the cab window, chimney, buffers and wheels to work with made this process much more difficult than I thought it would be, as the casing has numerous complex curves and planes. Eventually, with a lot of fiddling about with angles and curves, the locomotive arrived at its final shape. So, here we have No 6239 *City of Chester* working hard on the approaches to Tebay and the start of the climb to Shap summit. The feather of steam at the safety valves shows that it has a full head of steam and the coal pusher is in operation in preparation for the hard work ahead.

'DAYS OF RED AND GOLD'
30in x 20in

# 'EAST COAST TIME WARP'

Having built something of a reputation for historical accuracy in my railway paintings, it was with some initial misgivings that I contemplated a request from Silver Link Publishing Ltd to produce a painting for their 'past and present' book *The East Coast Main Line*, published in 1995 to mark the 60th anniversary of the introduction of the 'Silver Jubilee' train, and the 10th anniversary of the founding of the publishing company named after one of the 'A4' 'Pacific' streamlined locomotives that was built to haul it. The suggestion was that the painting should include 'A4' No 2509 *Silver Link*, in its original grey livery, hauling the 'Silver Jubilee', and one of the Class 91 electrics, to represent the 'past' and 'present' elements of the book. At first I found it quite difficult to come to terms with including both locomotives in the same painting, but the more I thought about it, the prospect of something 'different' took on a certain appeal.

Knowing little about the 91s, I duly arrived at Peterborough North station, camera in hand, with the intention of learning more about them. The visit had an almost instant reward. The second train to arrive included power car No 91001 *Swallow*, like *Silver Link* the first of its class. Some swift camera work recorded all the details of *Swallow* before it left for the north.

When considering how to arrange the picture, the similarity between the front-end shapes of the two locomotives became immediately apparent. It seemed a good idea therefore to place these shapes close together by having the trains travelling in opposite directions. In addition, this provided a convenient divide between the left and right halves of the painting, neatly separating the 'past' and 'present' elements. In order to fit both trains into the picture, I decided to have the 'Silver Jubilee' appearing round a curve as this allowed a composition without excessive width. I had some difficulty in finding a suitable location for the painting, so eventually and with some reluctance I decided to make the location imaginary.

In actually painting the picture, the 91 presented little difficulty – 30 or so photographs saw to that. As is almost always the case, however, what appears to be a straightforward project reveals more and more problems, the closer the subject is studied, and *Silver Link* was no exception. The locomotive featured differences in detail, making it unique among the 'A4s'. In addition, it underwent several changes, albeit of a minor nature, soon after building, and it soon became evident that some care would be needed to portray the locomotive correctly for the period chosen.

A search of my library revealed 20 or so photographs of *Silver Link* in its grey livery, all except one in black and white. All these photographs were subsequently used as references in putting together the 'A4' that appears in the painting. On leaving Doncaster Works in September 1935, the locomotive had a recessed front coupling, no front number, cast nameplates and a straight handrail along the side of the streamlined casing. Before entering traffic, however, the nameplates were removed and the words 'SILVER LINK' painted on the casing above the centre driving wheel. In 1936 it was further modified by having the recess around the front coupling removed and the handrail altered to clear the cab window. At the same time 'No 2509' was painted above the front coupling. The painting therefore shows *Silver Link* as it appeared after its 1936 visit to Doncaster Works.

Further touches included differences in track pattern for the two trains – flat-bottom track for the electric and bullhead rail for the 'Silver Jubilee'. The electric wires were conveniently 'lost' in the exhaust from the 'Pacific', and to balance the electric wiring one of the old 'somersault'-pattern signals was included, many of which were still in use during the mid-1930s.

'EAST COAST TIME WARP'
20in x 16in

# 'ECHOES OF THE PREMIER LINE'

Over the years I have been asked many times to reconstruct a scene. This one was more of a challenge than most. During recent years, Rugby Midland station has undergone a virtually complete remodelling and is almost unrecognisable when compared with the way it appeared 40 or 50 years ago, as most of the buildings that existed in the mid-20th century have now been demolished. The main station buildings remain, but the overall roof and supporting spans have long since disappeared, as have the goods shed and the signal boxes. Office blocks have now replaced some of the old houses in the vicinity, leaving very little to work on. I thought I knew quite a bit about Rugby, living only a few miles away. Indeed, on leaving school I worked for a time on the station before joining the Royal Navy in 1955, but memories fade in time and it wasn't long before I realised that this painting was going to be much more difficult than I had at first thought.

The painting was to feature one of Sir William Stanier's magnificent 'Princess Coronation' Class 'Pacifics' in the red livery that some of them carried during their last years in service. I suggested to my client that we might feature the 'Royal Scot', complete with its tartan headboard, not realising at the time that decent photographs of the Hunting Stewart tartan that forms the background are very difficult to come by. The locomotive itself was, thankfully, less of a problem. Two of the class, Nos 46240 *City of Coventry* and 46245 *City of London*, both of which carried the red livery, were kept in virtually immaculate condition during their later years, so the year 1960 was chosen, shortly before diesels took over the main passenger workings. The engine chosen was *City of London*, so I set to work to try and find all the details necessary to complete the picture. Finding references for the locomotive was the easy part. My library produced more than 20 good views, and much of the fine detail came from 40 or so photographs I took of *Duchess of Sutherland* at the Midland Railway Centre, Butterley. The 'Duchess' is, of course, a non-streamlined example, so some of the details had to be changed to turn it into a de-streamlined engine. Eventually, however, all the details were complete, right down to the positions of the overhead wires warning flashes, which were not always affixed in the same places.

A structure known locally as the 'wooden bridge' spanned all the tracks close to Rugby No 5 signal box, giving a superb panorama of the station complex, the old LNWR cottages at the end of Railway Terrace and Wood Street goods shed. My client had spent many hours spotting from this bridge, so this was the location chosen. The West Coast Main Line, strangely, runs almost east to west through Rugby. This posed problems with the lighting, as on a sunny day the view is against the light and would have meant that the whole of the main subject was in the shade. This was solved by choosing a showery day with lots of cloud and no shadows.

Research now began in earnest to find all the components of the painting. Eventually a hundred or so bits and pieces were gathered at all sorts of angles, but this still left several blanks and I was beginning to think that the picture couldn't be done. Then, one evening, on the internet, I came across a website that included several photographs of the track layout, including one that was the exact view I needed. It was taken in 1950 and included the whole station complex and virtually all its surroundings, but, unusually for Rugby, didn't feature any trains. I contacted the owner of the website, who was kind enough to send me a high-resolution print of the photograph, which, in conjunction with all the details I'd already found, I then used as the basis for the painting. On closer study, however, I realised that numerous changes had taken place during the ten years between the date of the photograph and 1960, when the painting was set. Many of the signals had been replaced and a number of sidings and crossovers had either been altered or removed altogether. The final details of these alterations came from a book long out of print on the railways around Rugby, lent to me by a friend. This included an aerial view of the western end of the station, which by sheer luck had been taken in 1961. This one reference completed the jigsaw and meant that the painting was a feasible proposition at last. I used to think I knew quite a lot about Rugby station. I can safely say that I know a lot more now!

'Echoes of the Premier Line'
36in x 24in

# 'ELEGANCE AND INDUSTRY'

I'm not sure whether this is the most complicated painting I've ever attempted, but it must be a very strong candidate. It was originally commissioned for the cover of *Encyclopaedia of the Great Western Railway* (published by Patrick Stephens Ltd in 1993), and the brief was interesting, to say the least. This was to include as much of the Great Western as possible in a single picture. The possibilities were almost endless, as the GWR had any amount of large, busy railway centres. What was really needed, however, was one that was concentrated into a fairly small space so that most, if not all, of it could be included in a painting. After a lot of searching, I came upon a picture of Newton Abbot. The Torquay Road bridge, which spanned all of the tracks just to the south of the station, provided a perfect viewpoint. Almost every aspect of the Great Western was included, from a complete station right down to a loading gauge.

Every Great Western train to the West of England, whether passenger or freight, had to pass through Newton Abbot, which at times during the summer holiday season became a real bottleneck, causing long delays to trains from both directions queuing for platform space. The station was completely rebuilt in the late 1920s, the new station opening in 1927. This eased the situation somewhat, but still meant that a lot of trains had to go through a fairly restricted space – not ideal for railway operation, but perfect for a painting. My library provided a fairly hazy photograph of the station from the road bridge, taken immediately after the station was rebuilt, almost unbelievably with not a single train in sight. The viewpoint was perfect, however, and provided the basis for the painting.

Since my early spotting days, the 'Star' Class, with their tall chimneys, large driving wheels and elegant proportions, had always been one of my favourites, so I chose one of them for the main subject of the painting, which is set in 1930, just after the station was rebuilt. Quite a number of 'Stars' were still to be seen during my early spotting days, but the one I chose for the picture was one of the original series, No 4010 *Western Star*, which was withdrawn as early as 1934. This represented the 'elegance' of the title. One of the ubiquitous '5700' Class pannier tanks was chosen to provide the 'industry'. No 5760 was built in 1929 and was allocated new to Exeter. I have a photograph of it taking a short freight along the sea wall towards Newton Abbot soon after it was built, so its presence at Newton Abbot is authentic.

The painting itself became a long and complicated exercise in perspective. The southern end of Newton Abbot station is on a fairly sharp curve. The tracks themselves are not parallel, but diverge to pass on either side of the signal box. This meant that every item of rolling stock and virtually every building had to have its own vanishing point. I ended up with about 30 different coloured spots all along the eye level, just above the signal box. To get the lighting I wanted, the picture was set in mid-afternoon. The shadows from the trees in Forde Park, to the left of the picture, fall across the tracks at this time of day and I felt that this feature added to the atmosphere of the painting. The Great Western changed its coach livery in 1928 from the very ornate fully-lined-out style to a much plainer version. Setting the painting in 1930 meant that I could include both varieties. Jim Russell's books on Great Western coaches provided details of some of the lovely outside-framed 'Siphon' vans that were so much a feature of the GWR, so I put a couple of these in as well. Various other oddities, such as one of the gas tank wagons that supplied outlying stations, were also included to complete the scene.

When the painting was almost finished, it was included in an exhibition at Old Oak Common sheds as a 'work in progress'. There were almost a hundred details still to be included; for example, the coaches were all 'hovercraft' with no wheels or bogies. It was closely inspected by several thousand people over a three-day period, but no one noticed!

'Elegance and Industry'
24in x 18in

# 'FIREWORKS AT CHILCOMPTON'

The Somerset & Dorset was, in many ways, a railway oddity. It had a complicated early history, which culminated in it being leased jointly to the Midland Railway and the London & South Western Railway in 1875. For 47 years, until the Grouping in 1923, these two companies ran the line with a great deal of success. After this it was administered by the LMS and the Southern, and even after nationalisation in 1948 it continued almost unchanged until it was finally closed in 1966. It was a line of great character, but operationally difficult as it included a huge climb over the Mendip Hills, 20 miles or so from Bath, with gradients of 1 in 50 for several miles from both directions. Some of its locomotives were designed especially for the line by the Midland Railway, with the Southern helping out in later years when traffic became intense during the summer months. In 1951 one of Bulleid's 'Battle of Britain' Class 'Pacifics' ran a series of trials over the

line and, although its suitability for the steeply graded route was perhaps debatable, four of the 'West Country' Class were transferred to the line soon afterwards. For the painting I chose No 34042 *Dorchester*, which was one of those with the shield-shaped town badge under the nameplate.

Chilcompton Tunnel, just short of Masbury summit, is almost at the top of the climb over the Mendips from Bath. It was originally single track, but another bore was built when this section was doubled, leaving a very characteristic pattern of brickwork on the tunnel face, which still exists today. I wanted to paint an evening scene, with the light reflecting off the side of the locomotive, and one of the four 'Pacifics' seemed just right for this purpose. A drive to the location confirmed that the light was right for the picture I had in mind and also revealed one or two amusing things about the tunnel. The railway had been closed for 25 years, but it was still possible to walk into the right-hand bore. Soot, at least 3 inches thick, still covered the roof and walls. Where the track had been there were a group of cattle pens, and the left-hand bore now had doors and a large sign that read 'The Midsomer Norton Rifle Club'. The tunnel is only 66 yards long, more of a long bridge really, but is on a fairly sharp bend and I remember wondering how the rifle club coped with their curved 'clubhouse'. At this point the trains, many of them double-headed, would have been making a maximum effort and moving quite slowly. In the painting, a previous train has started a fire on the embankment and some permanent way workers have arrived to assess the situation.

On the subject of fires, *Dorchester* was the subject of an amusing story told to me by Donald Beale and Johnnie Walker, two of the Somerset & Dorset's greatest characters and most famous drivers. They had charge of a southbound express and were climbing towards Masbury when Johnnie, the fireman, noticed smoke, shortly followed by flames, appearing from above the driving wheels. He debated whether to tell Donald, but as the flames got worse, decided he had no choice. He shouted to his driver to come and have a look. Donald's only comment was that it was nearly as bad as the one on his side! In the end, the train was stopped and the fire brigade had to be called to put out the fire in the boiler lagging.

'FIREWORKS AT CHILCOMPTON'
24in x 18in

# 'FIRST OF THE DAY'

Finding locations that feature both railways and canals is never easy, but the Oxford Canal provides some of the best opportunities. The canal and railway run in fairly close proximity from Oxford through Banbury to Fenny Compton, in Warwickshire. In most places along the canal the two transport systems are frustratingly close, but not quite close enough. I've found that there needs to be no more than a 20-yard gap between the two in order to feature both successfully, otherwise whichever is placed in the foreground overpowers the other. Just north of Oxford, however, near the village of Wolvercote, there is a location that satisfies all the criteria. It has a very convenient bridge, giving a panoramic view of the area known as Port Meadow with the 'dreaming spires' of Oxford in the distance.

For the locomotive, I chose one of the venerable 'Saint' Class 4-6-0s, No 2902 *Lady of the Lake*, which was a regular performer in this area in the late 1940s. I had always liked the class, with their tall chimneys and large driving wheels – they had a sort of 'leggy' elegance so typical of Great Western passenger locomotives. A total of 77 were built between 1902 and 1913. They were a merger of several different classes, so researching the 'Saint' Class can be something of a minefield. The first one, *William Dean*, was built in 1902; another 14 appeared soon after as 'Atlantics', but were later converted to 4-6-0s. Some had straight frames at both ends, while others had new front ends with outside steampipes and curved drop plates at the front only. Later examples had curved drop ends at both front and rear. Some had a lever reverse while others had a screw reverse. I'm sure that the only safe way is to find a photograph of the actual engine to be portrayed, taken at the right period, and so it was with *Lady of the Lake*. I found a single photograph, taken near Birmingham, showing the engine in GWR 1947 livery, which was just what I wanted for the painting.

For the narrow boats I chose a pair belonging to the Samuel Barlow Coal Company, *Little Marvel* and *Fair Trader*. The 'Sam Barlow' boats sported a particularly striking colour scheme, with the traditional roses and castles on the cabin doors and highly decorated tiller posts. The painting is set in 1947, when nationalisation was looming. Soon afterwards, all this finery was swept away in favour of a plain blue and yellow colour scheme. In the painting, the boats are taking a consignment of coal to the Oxford Brewery, and will eventually moor almost in the city centre.

The railway and canal run almost south to north through Wolvercote, so to get the lighting I wanted the time of day had to be set at early morning. The exhaust from the northbound engine is set against the dark cloud of a storm approaching from the west and, as a final touch, I included an angler unhooking his 'first of the day'.

'FIRST OF THE DAY'
30in x 20in

# 'GATEWAY TO SNOWDONIA'

This is one of those rare pictures that was not the result of a commission, but, in a sense, a memory of my own. During the years following the end of the war in 1945, when family holidays again became possible, I spent several summer holidays with my parents in Penmaenmawr, about 5 miles along the coast from Conway. The train always stopped at Llandudno Junction, from where you could see the beautiful view across the river estuary to Conway on the opposite shore, with the huge castle dominating the landscape, the little town crouched beneath its walls and the road and railway bridges keeping close company. During these holidays we often visited Conway and I soon got to know the place very well.

A few years ago I was asked to paint a picture at Deganwy, between Llandudno Junction and the Town station. Mary and I set out on the drive to Deganwy on a perfect summer's day to take location photographs. On arriving at Llandudno Junction and seeing the view of Conway across the river again after so many years, all the old memories came flooding back and I decided there and then that this was a view much too good to waste and that I would paint it as soon as I could.

It was three or four years later that the opportunity came. Both of us being well past retirement age, we decided between us to slow down somewhat. This meant that at long last I had some free time, so, taking advantage of a good weather forecast, we set off again for North Wales.

We parked at the Junction and I walked on to the station, ready with my camera. I had visions of just what the painting would look like, but arrived at the end of the down platform only to find that the view had been almost completely obscured by a very large supermarket and a new overbridge. This meant that an angle would have to be manufactured to get the view I wanted. As a first step I took 50 or so photographs of Conway from the causeway to the new road bridge and some more of the estuary, which is now heavily silted up, far more in fact than I remembered it.

After a great deal of searching the internet for pictures, track layouts and so forth of Llandudno Junction, I decided that the best angle would be from the site of the old No 1 signal box, which stood at the western end of the station. The signal box stood about 30 feet high and must have afforded a magnificent panorama of the river estuary, Conway and the hills beyond. Next, some motive power was required. My library turned up a huge variety of locomotives that had worked on the North Wales lines, but I decided eventually on a 'Britannia', mainly because I had never been asked to paint one. Holyhead shed had several allocated from new in 1954, all of which ran initially without names, and it was one of this group that I decided would appear in the painting. Considering that the 'Britannias' were supposed to be a standard design, painting one turned out to be a veritable minefield. A close study revealed that they had so many detail differences that hardly any two were alike. Eventually, though, I found a very clear photograph of No 70045 standing in Bangor station shortly before it was named, in July 1957. That settled the matter, so this is the engine that features in the final work.

Halfway through the painting I thought that perhaps there might be rather too much track, so I decided to fill it in somewhat. Another locomotive type that I'd never been asked to paint was the rather cute Ivatt Class 2 2-6-0, known in some circles as a 'Mickey Mouse'. No 46447 was a Llandudno Junction engine at about the time the painting is set, so it too appears, travelling light engine towards Llandudno Town to collect the daily pick-up freight. The 'Britannia' is coasting into Llandudno Junction with an early morning train from Holyhead to London.

'GATEWAY TO SNOWDONIA'
30in x 24in

# 'THE GREAT LITTLE TRAINS OF WALES'

One afternoon, some years ago, my wife Mary took a telephone call from a prestigious china company asking if I would paint a series of four pictures of Welsh narrow gauge railways to be featured on a set of limited-edition collectors' plates. Although I was well aware of the railways' existence and had visited some of them, I realised that I didn't know a great deal about them, narrow gauge railways not being a special interest of mine at the time. The telephone call took place in early September and the paintings were required for the following April. This was of course an opportunity much too good to miss, so I agreed to produce the paintings and set to work immediately to learn as much as I could about the narrow gauge railways of Wales.

We contacted some of the most likely candidates for timetables, only to find that they were all going to close for the winter in a matter of three or four weeks! In addition, the plate company wanted to approve sketches, which made the timescale even shorter. This created something of a panic, so we decided to drop everything and become commuters from Bedford to various points in Wales 'like yesterday'. On a couple of occasions we were unable to arrange accommodation at such short notice and ended up camping in the back of our Volvo estate car. The bubble wrap that we used to protect framed prints proved to be quite warm, if a little crackly! Over a period of two or three weeks we managed to visit all the chosen railways. The sketches for the four paintings were duly sent off to Stoke-on-Trent and were approved a short time later. The paintings were produced on time, and the following four pictures are the result.

## 'MERDDIN EMRYS AT TAN-Y-GRISIAU' (page 38)

No series of paintings of the Welsh narrow gauge railways would be complete without the Ffestiniog Railway. First incorporated as long ago as 1832, it has endured a long and chequered history, including a period of complete closure, before becoming the major tourist attraction it is today. The line is unique in pioneering the use of 'Double Fairlie' locomotives, and it is one of these engines that I chose to include in the

painting. No 10 *Merddin Emrys* was built by the Ffestiniog at Boston Lodge in 1879; it was the original 'Double Fairlie' and the natural choice for the painting.

I wanted to include the characteristic scenery of the area for each painting, but this proved surprisingly difficult on the Ffestiniog, bearing in mind that the final result had to be square. Eventually a location was found at the northern end of the line, near to Tan-y-Grisiau Power Station, looking over the hydro-electric reservoir towards Trawsfynydd. The best view was from halfway up the side of a very steep cutting. Finding a convenient tree to hang on to, I waited for the train to appear. I could actually hear it coming when several sheep decided to stand in the middle of the track. As the train rounded the bend the driver saw the sheep and gave a long blast on the whistle, whereupon *Merddin Emrys* disappeared behind a huge cloud of steam! By the time the steam had dissipated, the train had gone. Unfortunately, it was the last train of the day, so the next weekend it all had to be done again, this time with Mary on 'sheep watch'. The weather the following weekend was very much better and I got two excellent photographs of the train. *Merddin Emrys* appears in the painting in its 1989 livery of crimson with black and yellow lining.

## 'PRINCE OF WALES AT RHEIDOL FALLS' (page 39)

The Vale of Rheidol Railway, which follows a scenic route from Aberystwyth to Devil's Bridge, was acquired by the Cambrian Railways early in its existence, being absorbed into the Great Western in 1923. It originally had three engines, one of which was withdrawn in 1923 and another in 1934. Two more were built by the Great Western to the same design as the lone survivor, which had been built in 1902, and is the engine that appears in the painting. For much of the route it is difficult to see much in the valley due to the height of the trees, but there is one location on the upper section of the line, not far from Devil's Bridge, which, I was told, gives a superb view towards Rheidol Falls. Hoping that this might provide a suitable setting for the painting,

I set out to walk down the line from Devil's Bridge to find it. It proved to be a lot further than I had thought. After walking for about half an hour, I came across a photographer up a tree, complete with a tripod! He was perched above an enormous drop and looked as though he might fall off at any moment. He was looking for a new angle for next year's timetable. I decided there and then that I would be satisfied with any angle that didn't involve climbing a tree and he was able to tell me that the spot I was looking for was only a couple of hundred yards further on. He was exactly right and, quite suddenly; there was the view, just as I'd been told. A train was almost due and a quick scramble up the bank gave me a perfect viewpoint. The train appeared, hauled by No 8 *Llewelyn*. However, I knew that No 9 *Prince of Wales* had carried Cambrian livery for a while, a striking yellow with black and white panelling, so for the purposes of the painting the engine was changed and it is *Prince of Wales* that now appears.

## 'TAL-Y-LLYN AT QUARRY CROSSING' (page 40)

For the third in the series of paintings of Welsh narrow gauge railways I chose the Talyllyn Railway, a picturesque line that runs from Towyn, not far from Aberdovey, north-eastwards to Abergynolwyn. Having learned something from being forced to make two trips to the Ffestiniog Railway, this time we decided to make a weekend of it and spent an evening at Towyn talking to the staff and explaining our mission. The locomotive I wanted for the painting was No 1 *Tal-y-Llyn*. This little 0-4-2 saddle tank was built by Fletcher Jennings in 1865, making it the oldest working preserved locomotive in the world.

Having looked at the direction of the line, it was decided that the first train the following day would provide the best lighting. The weather forecast was good, but we were a little disappointed to be told that *Tal-y-Llyn* wasn't actually rostered for the following morning. Nevertheless, having obtained permission to 'trespass' at Quarry Crossing, we walked up the track from Dolgoch Falls on what promised to be a beautiful autumn day to wait for the train. The previous evening I had spent some time at Towyn shed taking detail photographs of *Tal-y-Llyn*, so that if the worst came to the worst I could 'transplant' it into the painting. When the train arrived, however, this proved not to be necessary – sparkling in the sun,

there was *Tal-y-Llyn*, looking as though someone had been up all night polishing! As a bonus the train included the lovely Corris Railway First Class coach, with all its intricate lining, next to the engine. The train made a perfect picture as it passed us at walking pace and I've always been grateful to the railway staff for making this part of the project so easy.

## 'THE COUNTESS AT CASTLE CAEREINION'
(page 41)

The last of the quartet of paintings featuring the 'Great Little Trains of Wales' didn't pose quite so many problems as the other three, mainly because the Welshpool & Llanfair Railway is far more accessible. It follows the main road west from Welshpool for much of its length and, after spending a day looking at possible locations along the length of the line, we decided on Castle Caereinion station as the setting for the picture. The railway does not have the spectacular mountain scenery of the other three, but nevertheless is very picturesque in a rather more gentle way.

The line was taken over by the Cambrian Railways early in its existence and was then absorbed into the Great Western in 1923. Two of the original locomotives built for the line are still in service; designed and built by Beyer Peacock, they entered service in 1903. After the Grouping they acquired GWR-type boiler fittings and became Nos 822 and 823 in the GWR list. The line closed in 1956 and the two locomotives were put into store. I remember seeing them in Oswestry shed in the late 1950s and I have some photographs I took of one of them on a low-loader at Didcot some years later. These photographs proved invaluable because at the time I was painting the picture neither of them was working. This meant an interesting exercise in perspective and foreshortening to 'transplant' one into the picture.

The line was re-opened in 1963 by a preservation society and is now a tourist attraction. The two original locomotives have been restored and renumbered No 1 *The Earl* and No 2 *The Countess*. For the painting I chose No 2, as I already had a 'No 1' for the series. For many years its name was placed on the side of the cab and, because it was too long to fit there, was shortened to *Countess*. It has now been restored to its full length and placed in its original position on the side tank.

'*MERDDIN EMRYS*
AT TAN-Y-GRISIAU'
16in x 16in

'PRINCE OF WALES
AT RHEIDOL FALLS'
16in x 16in

'*TAL-Y-LLYN* AT
QUARRY
CROSSING'
16in x 16in

'THE COUNTESS AT
CASTLE
CAEREINION'
16in x 16in

# 'HEAVYWEIGHTS AT SEATON'

Some years ago I was contacted by John Fry, a railway enthusiast and clinical biologist from Sussex, who was writing a book on the Bulleid 'Merchant Navy' Class 'Pacifics'. All of the class members were rebuilt from the original 'Spamcan' design to a more conventional form between 1956 and 1959, and he had searched without success for a photograph of both types together for the cover of his book. As no suitable photograph could be found, he asked me if I would paint a picture showing two 'Merchant Navies' in a typical setting, which would then be reproduced as the book cover. This seemed a fairly straightforward project, and we agreed that Seaton Junction would be a good choice of location as it had a very wide space between the platforms and plenty of space to include two trains. In the late 1950s it

At Seaton Junction station in the early 1990s, the view from the footbridge used for 'Heavyweights at Seaton' shows the overgrown platforms and all but one track lifted.

also had an absolutely superb LSWR signal at the eastern end of the station, which we decided was too good to waste and which duly appears in the painting. For the main subject we chose the 'Atlantic Coast Express', a famous train that ran in several sections from London to various places in Devon and North Cornwall.

Mary and I visited the location to find the station overgrown, with trees having taken root on the platforms and all the tracks except one having been lifted. The station buildings were still in position and being used by small businesses, but a real bonus was that the concrete footbridge, from where this view is taken, had not been demolished. This made all the background easy to reconstruct right down to the sign for the Shute Arms Hotel on the station approach.

My library produced several good photographs of the 'ACE' passing Seaton Junction, but every one showed the locomotive far too near to the camera. For the painting, I moved the express back a couple of coach lengths to leave room for the train in the opposite platform. This is the one that proved to be a problem. I could find not a single reference showing a 'Merchant Navy' at the right or even approximate angle, so in the end I 'built' one from the rails up by matching the wheels to a standard length of track and constructing the body of the engine from there. The parcels van was found during a visit to the Kent & East Sussex Railway, where it is preserved. To set the period, we chose No 35016 *Elders Fyffes*, which was rebuilt in April 1957, and No 35019 *French Line CGT*, which was rebuilt two years later, in May 1959.

Not long after the painting appeared on the cover of John Fry's book, we were contacted by a gentleman living in the North of Scotland, whose father had been the station master at Seaton Junction at the time the painting was set. He had grown up on the station and told us all sorts of stories about it. Perhaps the two most amusing involve the porter whose job it was to clear the adders off the platform, when they used to appear from a grassy bank and frighten the passengers. His special equipment for this consisted of a shovel and a pair of Wellington boots! The other concerned his mother's washing. Apparently I'd painted the train waiting in the platform in the exact position from where it used to blacken all her clean washing, which was drying in the station master's garden just behind the engine.

'HEAVYWEIGHTS AT SEATON'
24in x 18in

# 'INDIAN SUMMER'

Rugby had several classic 'spotting stations'. Possibly the best-known was at the northern end of Railway Terrace, where the road turns a right angle into Station Approach. Just on the turn there was a convenient gap in the wall almost opposite No 4 signal box, and close to where the old LNWR cottages once stood. From this vantage point the various activities at the western end of the Midland station

The view of Rugby Midland today from the end of the new No 1 platform at the corner of Railway Terrace, almost opposite the site of No 4 signal box. This is as nearly as possible the view used in 'Indian Summer'.

could be observed at a distance of only a few yards. Several thousand photographs must have been taken at this spot over the years, including quite a few of my own, so this was a comparatively simple painting to put together. The setting is the early 1960s, when the great train sheds were still in position, although by this time they had lost almost all of their glass panels and decorative woodwork.

The painting was commissioned by an enthusiast who had a strong childhood connection with Rugby. He wanted his memories reconstructed in a painting so that when the station was remodelled and the buildings demolished, he had a reminder of how it used to look. For the main subject he chose the last engine to be built by the LMS. This was 'Coronation' Class 4-6-2 No 46256 *Sir William A. Stanier FRS*, which entered service in December 1947, just a few days before nationalisation. This magnificent engine was the first of two developed and 'improved' by H. G. Ivatt, one of Sir William's successors. During its last few years in service it was restored to the glory of full LMS crimson lake livery, together with 15 other members of the class, and it is this that gives the painting its title. I've always regretted not having seen one of these superb machines in red livery, as I was in various parts of the world with the Navy up to the autumn of 1964. It has, however, been a real pleasure to have been able to paint several of them over the past 20 years.

In the painting the engine is shown re-starting a heavy down express from the main platform. The Stanier 'Coronations' always seemed to do everything required of them without all that much effort, but I'll never forget the great heavy 'thump' of their exhaust when starting a train or moving slowly. In the late 1940s and early '50s a group of us spotters used to meet at Kingsthorpe Mill, a location near our homes, on Sunday mornings. Kilsby Tunnel, on the main line, seemed to pose endless problems for the permanent way staff and the Sunday main-line trains were almost always routed through Northampton. We always knew when a 'Duchess' was going to appear round the curve towards Castle station from the sound of its exhaust, which was quite unlike any other engine. The GWR engines had their characteristic 'bark', the Southern 'Pacifics' their soft 'chatter', but nothing compared to the impression of sheer power conveyed by one of Sir William Stanier's masterpieces.

'INDIAN SUMMER'
30in x 20in

# 'LADY IN RED'

During our early spotting trips to Roade and Blisworth the appearance of one of Stanier's 'Princess Royal' Class 'Pacifics' always created something of a stir among the spectators. Perhaps because there were only 13 of them, including the 'Turbomotive', it was something to do with rarity value. Any or all of them could be seen on the West Coast Main Line in the early 1950s, however, as long as one was prepared to cycle to the lineside enough times. I believe, however, that it was more to do with the fact that they were such beautiful and elegant machines. They were very impressive because of their sheer length and the fact that they always seemed to be working harder and travelling slightly faster than they actually were because of their 6ft 6in driving wheels as compared with the 'Coronations', which had 6ft 9in driving wheels and therefore seemed to be making somewhat more leisurely progress. In the late 1940s and early '50s it was rare to see a clean one, as the LMS seemed to put a very low priority on keeping its engines in a decent state. My favourite, for some reason, was always No 46207 *Princess Arthur of Connaught*, possibly because of its rather strange name. How could a girl be called Arthur? It wasn't until many years later that I discovered that the wife of a Royal Duke also took his first name (as in Princess Michael of Kent), so the mystery was solved.

This was a picture I painted for myself. As luck would have it, No 46207 was one of the four that acquired LMS red livery late in their careers. All those that I remembered were either green or blue, and I was otherwise engaged in the Royal Navy when the red ones appeared, so I never actually saw one in its crimson lake colours, but they must have made a fine sight. When it came to painting one, however, *Princess Arthur of Connaught* was the natural choice. I wanted to show a train picking up water so I chose Bushey troughs as the location. The train would then be framed by the high overbridge that carried Oxhey Road over the railway just to the south of Bushey & Oxhey station. The troughs began just under this bridge so the train is shown just as the scoop hits the water, producing a cloud of spray under the leading coaches. The reflections on the wet sleepers that lined the troughs add (I hope) to the impact of the painting as a whole.

My last sight of one of these lovely engines was during the late summer of 1962, while returning to my then home in Montrose from Rosyth, having played in a cricket match for the Navy in Scotland. At Blackford, not far from Gleneagles, the car was held up at a lonely level crossing. It was late evening after a beautiful summer's day, with the light beginning to fade. Everything was quiet for a minute or two then quite suddenly a very fast fitted freight appeared from the direction of Perth hauled by a green 'Princess Royal'. I was so surprised that I completely forgot to take a note of the number, but subsequent reading suggests that it was probably No 46201 *Princess Elizabeth* on one of the up Aberdeen fish trains. Within what seemed like seconds, the train had come and gone. I never saw one again, and less than two months later all of them had been withdrawn. Somehow it seemed appropriate that my last sighting was of one of these magnificent engines disappearing into the dusk of a Scottish evening. Almost before the smoke and steam had dissipated, the crossing gates clanked open, the waiting cars moved off and the moment was over.

'LADY IN RED'
36in x 24in

# 'LEGENDS AT BATTLEDOWN'

The first Southern engine I ever saw was a 'King Arthur'. It appeared, seemingly out of nowhere, at Oxford one Saturday afternoon in 1950. It was our first visit to Oxford and, at the time, our little spotters' group didn't know about the through Bournemouth to Birkenhead trains, so its appearance was the cause of some excitement. The engine concerned was one of the original Urie 'Arthurs', No 30749 *Iseult*, which came off its train at Oxford and returned south later in the day.

For some time I had been looking for a chance to paint one of the first series of 'King Arthurs' when, about four years ago, I was visited by a gentleman who brought with him a copy of a *Meccano Magazine* dating from 1936. It contained a photograph of No 742 *Camelot*, on a West of England express, overtaking an electric train near Earlsfield. He wanted a painting taken from the cab of another 'King Arthur', running parallel with the express. The location seemed a little uninspiring, so I suggested that we look for a different setting for the picture. After some research I came across some photographs of Battledown flyover, near Basingstoke, which I thought would serve very well, so I sent him a couple of sketches outlining how the painting might finally appear. He liked the idea of setting the painting at Battledown, so I set to work, not realising that I had given myself a major problem. On visiting the location I found that the Salisbury and Bournemouth lines, although parallel, are not quite on the same level. The Salisbury line is super-elevated to take the curve under the flyover and is about 18 inches higher than the Bournemouth line. Constructing a second 'King Arthur' from scratch to appear slightly lower than the main subject proved a very interesting and, at times, frustrating exercise in perspective.

The other engine was to be No 453 *King Arthur* himself. This seemed reasonable, until I discovered that at the time the painting is set, *Camelot* was a Bournemouth engine while *King Arthur* was allocated to Salisbury. This meant that, strictly speaking, they were on the wrong tracks. I pointed this out to my client, but he preferred to leave the two engines as they were as he liked the square box over the cylinder of the older engine, rather than the later steampipe arrangement.

Battledown flyover is heavily staggered. This meant that the angle had to be carefully chosen so that the abutment on the far side could just be seen, otherwise it would look as though half the bridge had been missed out. I eventually got the angle I wanted by leaning out of a local train from Basingstoke to Micheldever and taking a series of photographs as the train approached the flyover. One lucky shot was just right and enabled me to complete the painting as it now appears.

'LEGENDS AT BATTLEDOWN'
30in x 20in

# 'LIGHT DUTIES'

A once top-line express locomotive on a four-coach local train gave this painting its title. The location is Knucklas, on the Central Wales line from Shrewsbury to Swansea. I knew of Knucklas and its impressive viaduct from previous visits to the line, but really needed something out of the ordinary by way of motive power to do justice to the painting. Most of the trains that used the line were hauled by Class 5 4-6-0s, 8F 2-8-0s and 2-6-4 tank locomotives. Late in their careers, however, a few of Sir William Stanier's 'Jubilee' Class 4-6-0s were transferred to Shrewsbury shed, having been displaced from their regular duties by diesels, so I chose one of these, No 45577 *Bengal*, which was known to have worked on the line in the early 1960s. During my spotting days, *Bengal* was known as one of the very rare 'Jubilees', as it spent most of its life in Scotland and was hardly ever seen south of the Border.

Mary and I set out very early one summer's morning on our usual location visit, expecting to find the place changed out of all recognition. We were pleasantly surprised to find the village, at first sight, much as it had appeared 40 years earlier. I wanted to include both the viaduct and as much of the scenery as possible in the painting, so we toured the village looking for a possible viewpoint. In the event, I had to climb a very steep field near the station to avoid a row of tall trees that had once been a low hedge. Some of the viaduct, which had once dominated the landscape, was obscured behind more trees growing on the embankment and it was obvious that some changes had taken place in the village itself. There seemed to be quite a few barn conversions and extensions to the houses, so it became necessary to find one or two pictures of Knucklas as it used to be in the 1960s in order that comparisons could be made. As a first step, we photographed the viaduct and almost every house in both

Knucklas and Heyop, a small village that appears in the middle distance. One or two views of Knucklas as it appeared in the early 1960s were eventually discovered, and I set to work to try and convert the village to its former appearance.

To get the lighting I wanted on the train and viaduct, the time was set at late morning. With the sun at a high angle, the shadows under the viaduct's arches give it a much more three-dimensional appearance. This meant that the time of year had to be somewhere near midsummer. The locomotive was withdrawn in October 1964, so setting the painting in June fitted the scenario very well.

The Shrewsbury to Swansea line west of Knighton is heavily graded, and watching trains there during the days of steam could be a rewarding experience. The line once carried a great deal of heavy freight traffic, and watching a heavy load with a Stanier 8F at its head struggling up the 1 in 50 gradient through Knucklas, often banked by another at the rear, both making a maximum effort, was a sight not easily forgotten. The train in the painting, travelling from Swansea towards Shrewsbury, is having a much easier time of it. It is shown with steam shut off and the fireman enjoying a breath of fresh air as it gently descends the gradient towards Knucklas station, ready for a possible request stop.

In this view of Knucklas Viaduct from above the station in the late 1990s, it can be seen that the station is now completely masked by trees, which were once a low hedge.

'LIGHT DUTIES'
36in x 24in

# 'MEMORIES OF METRO-LAND'

This painting was a commission, which, for once, posed none of the usual problems in putting a scene together. Although it is set in 1933, nothing much has changed, as the locomotives, the coaches and the station itself are all preserved. The station is of course Quainton Road, the home of the Buckinghamshire Railway Society. For a number of years Mary and I had been friends with Alan and Joan Newstead, who ran the shop at Quainton Road. It was Alan who suggested the idea for the painting because, although the society owned the station and the Metropolitan Railway 0-4-4 tank locomotive No 1, they could never put 'their train into their station'. The reason was that the line that passes through the site was, and still is, open and is used occasionally by trains from London to a landfill site north of Quainton Road.

'Met one', as it is known, had just been restored at Quainton when the painting was commissioned, and looked magnificent in its new red paint. The coaches, however, were at that time on the Keighley & Worth Valley Railway, which meant a long drive to get details of them. Quainton Road, as well as being a through station on the Great Central main line to London, was also the terminus of the Brill branch, which closed in 1935 and was worked week and week about by two ancient-looking Beyer Peacock 4-4-0 tank locomotives. One of these, No 23, is preserved in its original condition at the London Transport Museum in Covent Garden. Having decided to include this engine in the painting as well, I paid a visit to Covent Garden to photograph it. The museum's archive very kindly supplied me with some photographs of Quainton Road taken in the early 1930s, from which I was able to confirm all the details of the station, including the LNER posters and the large timetable on the wall of the station building. The 'Met' is quite well documented, so putting No 23 back into its 1933 condition was fairly easy.

The only task remaining was to think up a scenario for the picture. I decided on Derby Day 1933, featuring a special excursion for the races. The engine driver and the porter are seen selecting possible winners from the daily newspaper, while another member of the station staff waits for a couple of late arrivals to board the train before giving the 'right away' to the driver. No 23 is waiting to travel north to Verney Junction to collect a pick-up freight, from where it would meander down the line to London, eventually arriving at Neasden for a week's rest and servicing; this was a regular task for the Brill branch locomotives on change-over day. As a final touch I was asked to include one of the 'Quainton robins', which have made their home on the station for many years – he sits on the parcels barrow in the foreground.

'MEMORIES OF METRO-LAND'
36in x 24in

# 'MEMORIES OF SANDOWN'

It was in 1950 that I first saw anything of the railways on the Isle of Wight. This was on a day trip with my parents from Northampton by coach, which dropped us off in Southampton. From here we caught the ferry to Cowes, and I remember the ferry passing through the docks with huge liners seemingly on every side. My parents were content to relax on the seafront at Cowes, enjoying the sun and watching the ships go by, but, being by now a serious spotter, I couldn't wait to see some of the island's railways. I managed to find Cowes station and lost no time in booking a return ticket to Newport. This was the hub of most of the island's railways and soon I was happily ticking off the beautifully kept 'O2' Class tank engines, with their neat nameplates, which worked all the passenger trains. The railways on the Isle of Wight had a character all their own, and during my time in Portsmouth with the Royal Navy I took full advantage of the ferry between Portsmouth and Ryde to see more of the island.

It is quite unusual to find a lady commissioning a railway painting, but so it proved in this case. I was asked to paint a scene including Sandown station from a point near the level crossing where June and her two brothers used to put pennies on the line (didn't we all!). I'm not sure that the little 'O2' tanks did much of a job of flattening pennies, but the Stanier 8Fs that we in Northampton used certainly did. The location visit revealed that it would have been very difficult to make a picture from the area immediately around the level crossing, so we compromised by moving the whole scene a little further away to the embankment opposite Los Altos Park, which gave a good view of the station, with its unusual signal box on the station roof. The setting was to be during the early to mid-1950s, before the line to Newport was closed and the branch signal removed from the gantry in the painting. My client requested that her parents and brothers should also appear in the painting and that the locomotive featured should be No 21 *Sandown*. She provided me with a photograph of the family standing on a beach at about the right period, and we decided that placing them taking a walk in Los Altos Park would be the best way of getting them into the picture. The girl waving her handkerchief at the train as it passes on its way to Ventnor is June, who commissioned the picture – at the time she was about 10 years old. It seems to me very strange to think that we were both on the island at around the same time watching the trains, and destined to meet 45 years later to bring the whole scene back to life.

'MEMORIES OF SANDOWN'
24in x 18in

# 'OUT OF THE WEST'

This painting is one of my personal favourites, as it shows a Great Western express hauled by a clean locomotive travelling at top speed and a complete master of its task. It was commissioned by the owner of a gallery in Reading, who lived in the village of Basildon, only 300 yards or so from Goring troughs, the location of the painting. The view is from a road bridge that crosses the main lines towards the western end of the water troughs, giving a superb view of the troughs with the tracks disappearing into the distance and the surrounding countryside. He had spent many hours spotting from this bridge and wanted his personal memories of it reconstructed. He specified that the subject should be one of the re-built 'Stars', No 5084 *Reading Abbey*.

The Great Western main line from London to Bristol was originally laid to the broad gauge, and even now much of it retains a sense of great space – the distance between the two nearer tracks in the picture will be readily apparent. It was all this space that decided me to include another train. The water tank that supplied the troughs was an important feature, but to include part of this, as my client wanted, would have left a large blank area to the right of the picture. We decided that something by way of contrast to the express would complete the scene nicely. He suggested one of the '6100' Class 2-6-2 tank locomotives, which were quite common in the Reading area. This seemed quite straightforward, until a search of my library failed to find a single reference for the '6100' at the right angle. In the end I built one from the rails up by matching the wheels to the rail chairs and carrying on upwards from there! The 'Castle', on the other hand, posed few problems as there are quite a few books on this one class alone. One has to be careful with Great Western engines, however, as although at first glance they look alike, there are often numerous detail differences within a single class to trap the unwary. The rebuilt 'Stars', for example, retained their original frames when they reappeared as 'Castles'. They

had a 'joggle' to clear the front bogie wheels, which resulted in the inside cylinder cover being narrower than that of a standard 'Castle'. *Reading Abbey* was one of these engines, having been rebuilt in April 1937.

I have often been asked how to paint transparent smoke. This painting perhaps provides a good example. The wagons of the goods train were all painted and allowed to dry completely. The haze from the chimney of the 'Castle' was glazed over the wagons using a very thin mix of grey and 'Liquin' medium. It is quite easy to overdo this, making the underlying paint disappear. Should this happen, using a dry watercolour brush gently begin to remove the glaze, drying the brush at intervals, until the right amount of detail reappears. It is a process that is much easier than it looks – it just needs a little bravery to try it in the first place.

'Out of the West'

30in x 20in

# 'OUT TO GRASS'

The Edge Hill Light Railway was one of those wonderful anachronisms that were dotted around the English countryside during the first part of the 20th century, in many cases due to the activities of one Colonel Stephens. Opened in 1919, the EHLR was originally intended to be part of the war effort for the First World War, which, of course, had ended in 1918, so its original purpose was never fulfilled. Buried deep in the Warwickshire countryside, the railway featured a very steep incline for part of its length, which was worked by ropes and pulleys. The rest of the line consisted of several sidings, and a conventional steam-locomotive-worked connection with the Stratford-upon-Avon & Midland Junction Railway near Kineton. It had two locomotives, both Brighton 'Terriers', formerly Nos 73 *Deptford* and 74 *Shadwell*, which had been purchased direct from the LB&SCR. Their names were removed following purchase and they were renumbered EHLR Nos 1 and 2. The line carried on its activities transporting iron ore in a rather ramshackle fashion for about six years, closing suddenly over a weekend in 1925. The two locomotives were abandoned where they stood, lying derelict in the open and quietly rusting away for more than 20 years, finally being scrapped in 1946.

At a model railway exhibition I met a builder of O-gauge models who asked me if I'd paint him a 'Terrier' with a difference. He wanted rust and grime, and suggested the EHLR, which seemed to me to present the perfect

opportunity. We agreed the price and size of the painting and the commission joined what was at the time a fairly substantial waiting list. Some months later I had a telephone call from my client, who informed me that part of the front of his house had 'fallen off', and could he delay the painting until he had sorted out repairs? We agreed to put the commission on hold until his fortunes improved. Thinking this might be the end of the matter, I was surprised to receive a call about a year later, saying that repairs to his house had been completed and would I please go ahead with the painting straight away. I had, with some reluctance, to inform him that he was now at the back of the queue as I had some paintings to complete that could not be delayed, so we agreed that I would resurrect the commission at the earliest opportunity.

I then began some preliminary research and soon discovered that finding reference material was easier said than done as very few people seemed to know that the EHLR actually existed. Eventually I discovered several unattributed photographs of both locomotives in a miscellaneous collection in a book shop in Stamford. One of these photographs showed No 2 partially covered by a large tarpaulin, but at just the angle I wanted. For the painting, I 'moved' part of the tarpaulin to show more of the engine and, together with some of my own photographs of 'Terriers' taken at the Kent & East Sussex Railway, the painting was put together.

'OUT TO GRASS'
24in x 18in

# 'PENNINE STORMS'

For several years around the turn of the century, I provided the commentary on steam excursions run by a company based near Northampton, in succession to Mr Alan Pegler, the former owner of *Flying Scotsman*. The Settle & Carlisle line was a popular choice of destination, and on several occasions our motive power was provided by the National Collection's LNER 'V2' 2-6-2 No 60800 *Green Arrow*. At the time of writing, this superb locomotive has just been permanently retired and will now become a static exhibit. Perhaps this painting will serve as something of a memorial to its exploits over the previous 10 years.

The weather on the Settle & Carlisle can be very unpredictable, and sometimes downright hostile. Many of our trips were undertaken in late December, which might be thought of as tempting fate. We were, however, incredibly lucky with the weather on almost every occasion.

The excursion shown in this painting ran on 28 December 1999. *Green Arrow*, in immaculate condition, put up a splendid performance from Crewe to Carlisle via Blackburn and the Midland route, returning to Crewe via Preston and the LNWR route. I was the commentator on this train and well remember us being sidelined at Thrimby Grange, on the southbound climb to Shap summit, to let a couple of expresses pass. *Green Arrow* re-started 14 coaches from the loop with apparent ease.

In the painting the train is shown northbound at Grisedale Crossing, just after a water stop at Garsdale. *Green Arrow* is making a maximum effort to lift her 500-ton train up the last stages of the climb to Ais Gill. The exhaust follows the train, driven across the adjacent fields by a south-westerly breeze. Steam excursions on the Settle & Carlisle always attract crowds of photographers, whatever the weather. This one was no exception. All the photographers shown were 'transplanted' from

Chester General, where they were photographing another locomotive, *Canadian Pacific*, on another excursion a couple of years later.

This was one of those rare projects where all the components of the painting are preserved. The location and the farm appear just as they are today so all I had to do was to visit the location to check on the lighting for the painting. The support coach was photographed at York. The carmine and cream coaches were regulars on steam excursions at the time and I acquired quite a stock of photographs of them in various locations around the country. *Green Arrow* came from one of my own photographs, taken at High Dyke in the mid-1950s. By a lucky chance the angle was almost perfect and only needed minor changes in perspective to make it fit this picture.

'Pennine Storms'
36in x 28in

# 'RETURN TO BASE'

At a model railway exhibition at Farnham in October 1997 I had a long conversation with a gentleman who had spent quite a while making a very close study of the paintings on my display stand. His name was Brian Pickett and it emerged that he was the owner of 'Battle of Britain' 'Pacific' No 34067 *Tangmere*, which was in the process of being restored. His intention was to arrange an 'event', which he described with great enthusiasm. This would see the restored engine making a run on the Brighton to Portsmouth line when the restoration was complete, followed by a re-dedication ceremony at Chichester. He then asked me if I would paint him a picture of how the event might appear, setting the painting as near to the site of Tangmere air base as possible. Soon afterwards, Mary and I set off for Sussex to meet with Brian and search for a suitable location. We settled on a spot near the village of Oving, just to the east of Chichester, only a mile or two from Tangmere itself. The site had no means of getting above the level of the track, being in an open field, and I realised that an angle would have to be manufactured for the painting to give a view of the village and the South Downs in the background.

The painting was taking shape when I received a call to say that the restoration process had encountered some difficulties and would I mind putting the painting on hold for the time being. In the event, the partially completed canvas remained in my studio for the next six years, until I was

contacted by Brian in December 2003 to say that the locomotive's restoration had been completed and could I finish the painting as a matter of urgency as he had been diagnosed with terminal cancer and his health was failing very quickly. I contacted the clients on my commission list, all of whom agreed that I should 'drop everything' and finish the 'Tangmere' painting as soon as possible.

Some photographs of the completed locomotive and the Wessex Trains set of Mk III Pullman coaches were obtained, and it was at this point that the problems really started. I had painted *Tangmere* as it originally appeared, but the locomotive and tender now had so many detail alterations that a total repaint was going to be necessary. The time of year was to be changed from April to September and it quickly became clear that I would have to start the painting again, almost from scratch. In the event, I worked on the painting during every spare moment, including part of Christmas Day, and it was in early February 2004 that I rang Brian to tell him the painting was finished. I was told that he was now too ill to take phone calls and was passed to his son David to arrange delivery. The following day I met David at Wisley Services, on the A3 Portsmouth road, to deliver the painting, only to be told the terrible news that Brian had died that same morning. So, almost seven years after first commissioning the painting, Brian was destined never to see it, at least not in this world.

'RETURN TO BASE'

30in x 20in

# 'RETURN TO THE HIGHLANDS'

It was in 1989 that the Severn Valley Railway completed the restoration of Gresley 'K4' No 3442 *The Great Marquess*. I drove up to Bridgnorth to see it, resplendent in its brand new LNER livery, and made the most of the occasion by taking 50 or so detail photographs for a possible future painting. The locomotive's owner, the Earl of Lindsay, was seriously ill at the time, so arrangements were made to take *The Great Marquess* back to its old haunts on the West Highland Line to run a special train for him. This seemed to be a perfect opportunity to produce a painting of the engine amid the spectacular Highland scenery between Fort William and Mallaig, taking advantage of a short break in Scotland into the bargain. My wife and I set out on the 500-mile drive from the Midlands, breaking our journey on the way to take in the scenery around Loch Lomond. We eventually caught up with the engine at Mallaig. I'd had some thoughts of setting the painting there, but we arrived to find that Mallaig had changed radically from how I remembered it from when I'd lived in Scotland some 25 years previously. The harbour had been moved and a new road had appeared where the quayside used to be. There was no possibility of painting the picture I'd envisaged, so we set off back towards Fort William to find an alternative location.

About 15 miles south from Mallaig we came upon a spot where the railway crosses the road at the end of a small loch, dotted with islands. This is Loch Eilt, where the road and railway run along opposite sides, the railway on the southern side and the road to the north. The railway swings round a sharp curve at the western end of the loch, giving a superb view of the islands and the whole length of the water. The special train was being run on the following day, so we arranged our accommodation for the night, returning to the viewpoint the next day to wait for the train. On arriving at the place we had chosen, I was surprised to find a photographer exploring the same spot. He was becoming very frustrated because a group of large bushes was in the way of the view he wanted and he was leaning precariously over a ravine to try and avoid them. He asked me if I'd got any ideas, so I said I was going to move the bushes a few yards. He then asked me if I had a chainsaw!

Sometimes, artists have it easier than photographers. All I had to do was to paint the offending bushes a few yards away from where they really were. He, on the other hand, ended up halfway up the hillside, but nevertheless got a beautiful shot of the train, which I saw soon afterwards in the railway press. I have to admit to one more piece of artistic licence in this painting. The weather on the day before the special train ran was absolutely perfect, with bright sunshine and no wind. During the evening it began to cloud over and on the day of the special it was dull and drizzling. This didn't make for a good painting, so I moved the weather back to how it was on the previous day. Eventually the special arrived and I was able to get a lovely shot of it on the curve. This is the image that now appears in the painting.

The view of Loch Eilt for 'Return to the Highlands', with the offending bush in the left foreground.

'RETURN TO THE HIGHLANDS'
36in x 24in

# 'SHARING THE MOMENT'

This painting was the result of a commission from a client who requested a Great Western scene featuring a canal. The locomotive and boats were left to me, so I set out to try and find a suitable location. I knew of Little Bedwyn, a few miles from Hungerford, but wasn't very keen on setting the painting there because I knew that it would have to be taken back to the late 1920s, as the Kennet & Avon Canal went out of use and became derelict in 1933. After a great deal of trudging along canal towpaths in the depths of winter and finding nothing really suitable, I decided that it would have to be Little Bedwyn after all.

Mary and I set out for Little Bedwyn on a very cold winter's day, thinking that much would have changed in 60 years and wondering how it might be possible to put a painting together from what remained. I stayed on the road bridge, slowly freezing solid, taking photographs of the passing trains, mainly HS125s, in order to get the scale correct. My wife, on the other hand, was knocking on doors trying to find someone in the village who might know something of the history of the place. She soon struck gold. A Mr & Mrs Cooper, who lived in Lock Cottage, just out of view to the right of the scene, owned some black and white 35mm slides of very old postcards. One of these slides was a view of Little Bedwyn from the road bridge, showing heaps of mud along both sides of the canal, which we were able to date to 1929. During that year the Great Western Railway, which owned the canal, was taken to court by boat users, who alleged that there was not enough water and that their boats kept grounding. The GWR lost the case and was forced into a major dredging operation. This set the painting perfectly and, from looking at this one slide over a period of three months through a jeweller's lens, I was able to reconstruct the village exactly as it was in 1929. There were many detail differences, as might be expected: trees that had been destroyed by Dutch elm disease, houses that had been thatched and were now tiled, cottages that had been demolished, the footbridge, which had been changed from a wooden to a concrete construction, houses with extensions, chimneys that had changed position, and so on.

Now, a boat and a train were required. As mentioned earlier, I have always admired the Great Western 'Saint' Class, with their simple lines and 'leggy' elegance, and this was my chance to put one into a picture. I chose No 2982 *Lalla Rookh*, named after a character in one of Sir Walter Scott's novels, to double-head one of the then new 'Castles'. For the latter I chose No 4093 *Dunster Castle*, the first of the class to receive a 4,000-gallon tender. The boat might have been more of a problem, but the National Waterways Museum came up with the goods in the shape of a Kennet barge called *Unity*, which belonged to the boat-builders Robbins, Lane & Pinnegar and was known to be the last boat to use the canal before it became derelict in 1933. Only two photographs of *Unity* are known to exist, both of the stern. This meant that in the picture it had to be going north, towards Hungerford. It was a very large boat, 67 feet long and 13ft 9in wide, and would only just fit into the locks on the canal. It was hauled by two heavy horses, and here again the National Waterways Museum at Gloucester came to the rescue. They had a very impressive Shire horse, Peter, who was walked round their yard for me to photograph. He now features twice in the painting. It then only remained to set the time of day. The main line through Little Bedwyn runs almost north to south, so to get the lighting angle I wanted I chose 10 in the morning. As a bonus, I was able to include the shadows from some large trees just out of view on the right.

Years later, after the painting had been published, we had a telephone call one evening from a gentleman with a pronounced Canadian accent, who proceeded to tell us all sorts of detail about Little Bedwyn village. He had been born there and was now travelling the world on behalf of Radisson Hotels, so we were somewhat amazed when he told us that, 50 years before, he had been the village poacher!

'SHARING THE MOMENT'
30in x 20in

# 'SOUTHERN SUBURBIA'

This painting was the result of a commission from a client who was then living near Guildford. He and his wife came from the Coulsdon and Purley area and the brief was to include a brand new 'Schools' Class locomotive passing through Coulsdon North station. The locomotive he wanted was No 915 *Brighton*, which was allocated to Eastbourne shed from new in May 1933. This effectively set the period of the painting, so I then set about researching the subject. A 4-LAV electric unit was also to be included. These units were also new in 1933 and here I have to admit that I knew nothing about them at all, being very much steam-orientated. A search through my library turned up a few photographs of Coulsdon North, including one or two taken in the 1930s, but I was unable to find sufficient detail to even make a start on putting together a painting. We both visited the location to find that, although the footbridge remained, there was nothing else left of Coulsdon North station other than the four nearest tracks in the painting.

The view from the footbridge looked promising as it would also have included the Tattenham Corner branch, which ran alongside the main line before curving off towards Epsom. Unfortunately, nothing remained of this feature either. In addition, Coulsdon itself was invisible behind a row of very tall trees and an industrial estate. I took some photographs of what remained of the scene, mainly to set the lighting, and began to wonder where to go next. My client eventually came to the rescue with a highly detailed railway map of Coulsdon North, which was dated 1934. A close study of this map revealed the positions of all the signals and crossovers, the Tattenham corner branch, the two signal boxes and a large part of Coulsdon itself. The only feature that appeared in photographs taken in the 1930s and those I took on the location visit, apart from the four remaining tracks, was a large poplar tree, which appeared in the middle distance. The map also showed an electric relay station just to the south of the main-line signal box, which we later found was not built until 1934.

I now had enough material to make a start on the painting, which was obviously going to be somewhat complicated. The method I used was to mark the spot on the footbridge that was the exact viewpoint as it appeared on the map, then, with a straight edge, line up all the houses visible in Coulsdon one by one. The row of houses adjacent to the Tattenham Corner branch is called Windermere Avenue. I have never been closer to it than the old footbridge, but I feel that I know it very well! The poplar tree was invaluable in setting the distances from the footbridge. Other details, including all of the signals and the Tattenham Corner branch station and signal box, were gleaned from the photographs in my library, and the painting began to take shape.

It had been decided that the 'Schools' Class locomotive would be shown going away towards London. This left a rather large area of tracks near to the main signal box, which really needed to feature another train. My client and I agreed that a Newhaven boat train hauled by a Marsh 'Atlantic' would serve very well, so No 2421 *South Foreland* duly filled the gap. Two-thirds of the way through the painting I happened to be at Quainton Road and found a beautiful photograph of a Marsh 'Atlantic' passing through Coulsdon, taken from platform level. This showed that the platforms had lawns only a short way back from the platform edges. It also included the fence between the platform and the embankment, the platform lamps and the station nameboard. All these details were included in the painting, which was completed with only one further problem. My client had wanted his 'Schools' to be in malachite green. This would have been totally incorrect for the 1933 period as these locomotives were turned out in London & South Western dark olive green with black and white lining from new. By the time *Brighton* appeared in malachite green, it had been transferred to the eastern section and was working between London and Ramsgate. As a final touch I decided to add a feature to the long fence. By chance, a friend was fitting a wardrobe in our house, so I gave him a large sheet of hardboard and a paintbrush and photographed him from an upstairs window with instructions to look as though he was painting a fence. He now appears twice in the finished painting.

'SOUTHERN SUBURBIA'

24in x 18in

# 'STAR QUALITY'

Ever since my first visit to the Great Western, at Banbury in 1947, I have had an affection for GWR locomotive designs, and my particular favourite has always been G. J. Churchward's 'Star' Class. With their clean and elegant lines, slim boilers and polished copper and brass, they always seemed to me to exemplify just how an express passenger locomotive should look. To my mind, they had real 'Star Quality'. Just before nationalisation, about 50 were still in service, although many were almost at the end of their working lives. They were, in the main, very long-lived engines, first appearing as long ago as February 1907. One of the original batch, No 4003 *Lode Star*, is preserved at York in the National Collection and this is the engine I chose to paint.

A search of my library for a typical Great Western rural station revealed quite a few candidates, but eventually I settled on Patchway, about 6 miles north-west of Bristol, which seemed to 'tick all the boxes'. The location visit proved interesting mainly because it took so long to find the station, or what was left of it. We must have driven past it several times, not realising that it was still there. The rural scene that appears in the painting has now virtually disappeared and the station is surrounded by chemical storage facilities and a large bus depot. The platforms and half the footbridge are still there, but all the other features of the station have been swept away.

I wanted to set the picture in the early 1930s, to my mind the golden age of the Great Western, but it was immediately obvious that the present Patchway station wasn't going to be of much use. Fortunately, I found several photographs of the station in my library, which, when compared with my location photographs, gave me all the details I needed. Patchway stands at the summit of the climb from the Severn Tunnel and has a distinctly odd track formation. The track through the down platform is level. The up line, however, comes up the steep climb from the tunnel, creating an optical illusion when viewed from the platforms.

Getting *Lode Star* and its train into period was comparatively easy. The Great Western has always had an enormous following among railway enthusiasts and is particularly well documented. Details of locomotive liveries are readily available and the locomotive itself was available for detail photographs. Jim Russell's books on Great Western coaches helped put the train together. In the completed painting, *Lode Star* is shown at the summit of the climb from the Severn Tunnel with an express from South Wales to Paddington, having just shut off steam for the junction at the eastern end of Patchway station. On the platform a well-dressed gentleman of the time watches as the train sweeps past, while a porter loads some pigeon baskets and parcels that have been dropped off an earlier train.

The remains of Patchway station, 6 miles north-west of Bristol, in 2003.

'STAR QUALITY'
36in x 24in

# 'STRAWBERRIES FROM SOMERSET'

This is another instance where I was asked to reconstruct a personal memory. It was commissioned by a gentleman who, as a small boy, had lived in Cheddar – he appears in the painting standing with his mother on the far platform. His father, who was the local coal merchant, is standing by the fence on the near platform. For some years he went to school in Wells by train. The GWR 'Bulldog', No 3371 *Sir Massey Lopes*, although allocated to Westbury, was a regular performer on the Cheddar Valley line and he saw it on many occasions at Wells.

Cheddar station itself was a beautiful example of a design by the great Isambard Kingdom Brunel for the Bristol & Exeter Railway, typical of

many across Somerset during the mid-19th century. The line has now been closed for many years, but the station house and platforms remain much as they were, although the characteristic Brunel roof has now been demolished. My wife and I spent a very pleasant afternoon taking photographs of what remained, as references for the painting. We were delighted to be allowed on to the platforms, to find them peopled by rows of carvings of dragons and gargoyles, as the remaining parts of the station are now used as a workshop by the stonemasons from Wells Cathedral, a few miles away to the south-east.

In order to set the painting so as to coincide with my client's journeys to school in Wells, we chose 1939. This meant the locomotive had to feature the 1934 GWR livery of unlined green, with a painted-over safety valve and the 'shirt button' monogram on the tender. In keeping with the character of the line, I painted it somewhat work-stained. For the coaches I chose one of the then fairly new 'B' sets. At that time the area around Cheddar was well known for its strawberry fields, so this was chosen as the theme for the painting. The 'Bulldog' is collecting a 'Siphon G' van full of strawberries from Cheddar station, which will shortly be attached to the front of the 'B' set and taken off to Yatton and thence to Bristol for distribution to markets as far away as Covent Garden. There was one aspect of this painting that I really didn't understand. Why didn't the smoke stains on the front of the station's overall roof line up with the obvious outlets just above them? I spent ages checking the perspective in every way I could think of, but it just refused to come right. Then it dawned. The station had originally been broad gauge and some alterations must have been made to the platforms following the change to standard gauge in 1892, resulting in the misalignment shown in the painting.

'STRAWBERRIES FROM SOMERSET'
30in x 20in

# 'SUMMER AT SALTERN COVE'

Late one evening I received a telephone call 'out of the blue' from a gentleman in Cornwall. 'I'd like you to paint me a picture,' the voice at the other end said.

'All right, what would you like?' I asked.

'I'll leave it to you.'

'Come now, you must have some idea.'

'Oh, something set in the West Country, perhaps with a Cornish connection – how about a "Star"?'

The GWR 'Star' Class, being one of my favourite engines, made this an exciting proposition, so we agreed on the details and I set to work to find a location. Eventually I chose the stretch of line between Paignton and Churston, on the Kingswear branch. This was an unusual line as, despite being a single-track branch, it could take the heaviest locomotives. It was quite normal to see 'Kings' and 'Castles' there as well as the other GWR express passenger types. The nearest 'Star' name I could find with anything approaching a Cornish connection was the last member of the class, No 4072 *Tresco Abbey*, Tresco being in the Scilly Isles. We agreed that this would be acceptable and Mary and I set out to reconnoitre the locations.

After driving down most of the side roads between the main Paignton to Churston road and the coast, we eventually found Saltern Cove. Here the railway passes through a shallow cutting and along the top of a cliff, giving a commanding view over the expanse of Torbay. This looked perfect, so we took a lot of location photographs and, armed with these and several photographs from my library, I started putting the painting together.

After about two weeks it became evident that a big mistake had been made. The lighting wasn't working, and needed to be changed from mid-morning, when we took the location shots, to mid-afternoon. I couldn't work out the complicated shadows on the rocky headlands in the background, so there was nothing for it but to make another trip to Devon. This time, on a beautiful summer's day, we waited until the shadows were right for the painting. This turned out to be at around 3.00pm, so another set of location photographs were taken and we returned home to try again. On our second trip the cutting was full of marbled white butterflies and I couldn't resist putting half a dozen into the painting.

All went well until the painting was almost finished. Then I got another telephone call. Would I mind putting two boys and a dog somewhere in the picture? This posed something of a problem as they had to be somewhere in the foreground to make them big enough to be seen. I had to take a little artistic licence and alter the shape of the bank to give them something to stand on. I also gave them a bush to hide behind, as they are trespassing on the railway at that point.

*Tresco Abbey*, the engine in the painting, is shown as it appeared in the early 1930s. It was built in February 1923 and withdrawn in March 1938, reappearing the following month, still with its original name, as a 'Castle' Class locomotive, No 5092. In both guises it gave 40 years of service, finally being withdrawn in July 1963.

The Paignton to Kingsbridge branch at Saltern Cove, with Tor Bay in the background. This stretch of line is now part of the Paignton & Dartmouth Steam Railway.

'SUMMER AT SALTERN COVE'
30in x 20in

# 'THE HAYMARKET WANDERER'

A Scottish engine, in immaculate condition, in an unusual location, on a freight train. A very strange set of circumstances, but nevertheless a personal memory of the gentleman who commissioned this painting. Then a schoolboy, he saw this engine in its blue livery, travelling slowly south through Welwyn Garden City, from the top of a bus in June 1951. He wanted the scene reproduced as he remembered it, but research showed that too much had changed at the original scene to make this a possibility. I suggested Welwyn North as an alternative, as the train would have had to pass through this station to have got to where he saw it. This was agreed, and I went to Welwyn North to have a look at the location and to take some photographs.

Welwyn North is buried in the Hertfordshire countryside, sandwiched between one of the Welwyn tunnels and Welwyn Viaduct, and proved surprisingly difficult to find by road. After some searching, I found the station and tunnel much as they were in the early 1950s, except for the disappearance of the signals and the siding to the left of the picture. My client had some photographs of the scene and a search of my library revealed several more, so it wasn't difficult to restore the station to its former appearance.

I was, to say the least, intrigued by the sighting of an Edinburgh-based 'Pacific' on a freight train so far away from its usual haunts. The engine concerned was 'A1' Class No 60161 *North British*, from Haymarket shed. A little subsequent 'digging' through the records soon provided an explanation. Designed by A. H. Peppercorn, the last Chief Mechanical Engineer of the London & North Eastern Railway, No 60161 was the penultimate member of the class, appearing from Doncaster Works in blue livery in December 1949. It ran nameless until June 1951 when, following a visit to Doncaster for repairs, it appeared with the name *North British*. Its sighting at Welwyn soon afterwards meant that it was almost certainly on a 'running-in' turn from Doncaster.

With the mystery solved, the painting began to take shape. My client insisted that the patch of bare chalk on the cutting just to the right of the tunnel mouth should appear in the painting. This has been a feature of Welwyn North for many years and still exists today. To include this meant that the scene had to be set well back from the northern end of the platforms, otherwise it would have been masked by the exhaust from the engine. This left a large area of the down platform to deal with. This was solved by setting the scene on a showery day and including reflections of the signal gantry and trees on the wet platform surface.

The title of the painting refers not only to this sighting of *North British* so far from Edinburgh. On its return to Scotland it spent only three months at Haymarket before being transferred to Polmadie shed in Glasgow. It then spent the next 21 months working on the West Coast Main Line before returning to Haymarket in June 1953. Its wanderings then ceased and it remained based in Edinburgh until it was finally withdrawn from service, in October 1963, after a working life of less than 14 years.

'THE HAYMARKET WANDERER'

18in x 14in

# 'THE HIBERNIAN CONNECTION'

This painting, by sheer coincidence, features the very first locomotive I collected as a nine-year-old spotter, but not in the form in which it appears in the picture. A walk with a couple of school friends one Sunday to Kingsthorpe Mill, near my home in Northampton, produced a northbound express, diverted round the Northampton loop and hauled by an unrebuilt 'Royal Scot' 4-6-0, No 6141 *The North Staffordshire Regiment*. I remember that the locomotive was absolutely filthy, so much so that it was quite difficult to read the

number. Nevertheless, this was the start of my passion for railways, which has lasted from that day to this.

Many years later, I was asked by a client who had strong childhood connections with Rugby to paint a scene from the 'wooden bridge' near No 5 signal box. He wanted 'The Irish Mail' hauled by a 'Royal Scot', and specified No 46141 *The North Staffordshire Regiment* as the locomotive to be featured. At the time the painting was to be set, during the late 1950s, the 'Scot' was a Carlisle Upperby engine and not one that would normally have been found on a Holyhead train. He was most insistent on this particular one, however, so we decided that for the purposes of the painting it must have been 'borrowed' from its home shed or perhaps had not yet returned north after a light repair at Crewe Works.

The view from the 'wooden bridge' that we settled on left rather a lot of trackwork in the foreground, so I suggested that a freight train on one of the nearer tracks would improve the composition. This was agreed, so I included an LNWR 'G2a' Class 0-8-0, widely known as a 'Super D'. They were a very long-lived class and numerous examples were still running in the Rugby area in the late 1950s. 'Running' is perhaps something of a misnomer: I can't recall ever seeing one moving at more than about 10 miles an hour, and most of them seemed to leak steam from every available orifice. The one in the painting has just re-started a heavy freight for the Birmingham line and I couldn't resist giving it its characteristic steam leaks. The 'Irish Mail' has also just re-started and is about to enter the 25mph speed restriction imposed in connection with the building of the flyover taking the up Birmingham line over the Trent Valley Line, which was under way at the time.

The great train shed of Rugby Midland station appears in the distance and, beyond that, three of the 600-foot Hillmorton radio masts, which were such a landmark in the area. Like so much of the railway infrastructure around Rugby, they too have now disappeared.

'THE HIBERNIAN CONNECTION'
30in x 24in

# 'THE LAND OF LOST CONTENT'

To any railway enthusiast, this scene needs little by way of introduction. It is of course Ais Gill, with the mass of Wild Boar Fell looming in the background. It marks the summit of the famous 'long drag' on the Settle & Carlisle line and is the highest main-line summit in England. The line was built by the Midland Railway at enormous cost, due to the numerous viaducts and tunnels along its length, and opened in 1875. North of Carlisle, the Midland trains used the Glasgow & South Western Railway route to Glasgow and the North British Railway route to Edinburgh. The latter was known as the 'Waverley Route', and it is from that line that the train acquired its name. Formerly known as the 'Thames-Forth Express', the 'Waverley' name dates from 1957. It was fairly short-lived, as the connection from Carlisle to Edinburgh disappeared with the closure of the 'Waverley Route' in January 1966.

Given favourable weather conditions, the Settle & Carlisle is a photographers' and artists' paradise, with spectacular scenery on every side, and several of my paintings have been set there. I particularly like the shape of Wild Boar Fell, so when the chance came to paint a Leeds-based 'Jubilee' Class 4-6-0, Ais Gill was the natural choice for the setting.

The artist has several advantages over the photographer when it comes to portraying railways. Weather conditions can be manufactured,

angles can be changed and appropriate motive power supplied at will. So it is with this painting. The viewpoint is in mid-air, as I thought a slightly elevated view would give a better composition and show more of the surrounding countryside, including the hills beyond Wild Boar Fell.

The 'Jubilee' for the main subject of the painting was specified as No 45608 *Gibraltar*, based at Holbeck shed and a regular performer over the Settle & Carlisle. Double-heading was fairly common over the route in the late 1950s, so as a bonus I decided to add another 'Jubilee' as the train engine, this time No 45729 *Furious*, from Kingmoor shed, Carlisle. Both are working hard, having just completed the northern half of the 'long drag', but are about to ease off for the downhill run towards Leeds.

A close study of the two engines revealed several detail differences between them. The most noticeable are the different tenders and the cab-side numbers. Scottish engines were immediately recognisable, as the cab numbers were much larger than those used in England. To add a splash of colour to the scene, I painted the leading coach in the old carmine and cream livery, which had been superseded by maroon in 1956.

The title of the painting is taken from a short poem by the Shropshire poet A. E. Housman. To anyone who cares to look it up, its meaning to a railway enthusiast will be obvious.

'The Land of Lost Content'
30in x 20in

# 'THE MAIL ALWAYS GETS THROUGH'

This painting shows one of my very rare departures from the steam railway scene. In 1999 I was commissioned to produce a painting that was to be used as the Post Office corporate Christmas card. The brief was to include a Post Office and one of the then new Class 325 electric trains that carried mail up and down the West Coast Main Line. Getting detail photographs of a 325 proved very interesting. Mary and I were given the run of what was then the brand new Post Office depot at Warrington. We spent a fascinating if somewhat chilly day there, watching the comings and goings of the trains. Finding a Post Office within sight of a suitable railway scene, however, proved to be no easy matter, but my contact, Alan Williams, one of the Post Office directors, told me that he had seen one almost next to the track from a train on the way to Manchester. The train had been diverted via Crewe and all he could remember was that it was 'on the right-hand side of the train, somewhere between Stafford and Crewe'. The fact that he was able see the Post Office sign from a fast train meant that it must be very close to the track and appeared to be a good prospect, but left a fair amount of ground to cover, so Mary and I set off to try and find it.

After a couple of days spent driving around the by-ways north of Stafford and getting absolutely nowhere, I decided the only way was to get on a train myself and see if I could spot it from there. The following day I boarded a northbound express at Rugby. The train stopped at Stafford and, as it left, I waited at the ready by an open window. The train accelerated quickly to 70mph or so, and thus far I'd seen nothing, then suddenly, next to an overbridge, the Post Office flashed past. I had a fleeting impression of a white building that looked like a large cottage, only a few yards from the main line. I estimated that it was about 6 or 7 miles north of Stafford, so on returning home it was out with the map and back in the car for a second attempt to locate it.

This time the hunt was successful. The location turned out to be Cotes Heath, near Eccleshall, and the Post Office was indeed right next to the railway, standing all by itself with no other buildings in view. I began to take location photographs, but it then occurred to me that I must look a bit suspicious 'casing the joint' as it were, so I introduced myself to the Postmaster, Harry Peacock, who, once he knew what was afoot, was very helpful and suggested that I wait for the mail collection van, which was due in about an hour. On returning home I rang my contact to say that I had found the Post Office, which was perfect for the painting. He had by then decided on a title and asked if I could provide some appropriate weather conditions. We decided that a snow scene would be in keeping with the theme of the picture, so this is how it appears in the finished painting, complete with the Post Office van and a couple posting their Christmas mail. They have no idea that they are featured. Perhaps if they see the book, they might even recognise themselves.

'The Mail Always Gets Through'
30in x 20in

# 'THE SCOTTISH PREDATOR'

This painting gets its title from the name of the locomotive. The 'Wolf of Badenoch' was one Alexander Stewart, 1st Earl of Buchan. He was the fourth son of King Robert II of Scotland and younger brother of King Robert III. Born in 1343, he spent a large part of his life rampaging across northern Scotland, supported by an army of renegades and wild Highlanders. He was excommunicated by the Bishop of Moray over a marriage dispute and retaliated by sacking the towns of Forres and Elgin, burning down Elgin Cathedral in the process. He was imprisoned by his brother, King Robert III, and made to do public penance, afterwards being pardoned. He is reputed to have died in 1394, after playing chess with the Devil, and is buried in Dunkeld Cathedral, Perthshire. He was otherwise known as 'The Celtic Attila'.

The painting was commissioned by a friend in Scotland who has an enormous enthusiasm for these lovely 'P2' 2-8-2 engines. They were large and very impressive and were the only eight-coupled express locomotives built for a British railway. Designed specifically for the Edinburgh to Aberdeen line, only six were built; the first two appeared in 1934, and four more in 1936. After alterations to the first two, they all bore a superficial resemblance to the 'A4' 'Pacifics'. They are a real 'minefield' for the artist and modeller, however, as no two were exactly alike. *Wolf of Badenoch*, for example, was distinguished by a longer firebox and extra washout plugs with domed covers.

The location visit for this painting proved more than usually interesting. Mary and I decided to combine looking for locations with a short holiday in Scotland at Banchory, on Deeside. After meeting up with my client, we toured most of the main line between Arbroath and Aberdeen in search of a suitable location for the picture. He particularly wanted a good view of the four driving wheels. This, for one reason or another, took out quite a few of the locations we found. Eventually we settled on Lunan Bay, between Arbroath and Montrose, strangely enough only about 3 miles from where I lived for two years during my time in the Navy. The site is now very overgrown and some of the features of the countryside had to be gleaned from an Ordnance Survey map, particularly a small viaduct that can no longer be seen from the painting's viewpoint. I was requested to include some red grouse, but as I'd never seen one in this area, I decided to check up on their habitat. They live up on the moors, feeding on heather shoots, and are not seen near the coast. In the end we compromised with some partridges, which are taking off with their characteristic whirring of wings, having been startled by the train. The train itself has steam shut off and is slowing down to collect the staff for the single-line section just to the south of Montrose. The small coaster anchored in Lunan Bay is the *Lochside II*, which for many years transported cargoes of beer from a brewery in Montrose to various ports in eastern Scotland and as far away as Newcastle-upon-Tyne.

Once all the research had been completed, the painting was quite straightforward, with the exception of the lining on the locomotive. Photographs of 'P2s' are quite rare as they only ran in the condition illustrated for a few years, and a lot of searching was necessary to see just where the lining went. They were all rebuilt during the war years, reappearing as rather ungainly 'Pacifics'. They must have provided quite a spectacle in their grass-green livery. I would have loved to have seen one.

'THE SCOTTISH PREDATOR'

30in x 20in

# 'THE SUMMER OF '47'

My wife and I chanced on this lovely rural scene one evening on a drive home from visiting my parents in Somerset. The location is Lower Heyford, on the line from Banbury to Oxford. The Oxford Canal and the railway are very close together at this point and, as we took a short break from our journey, Mary suggested that it would be a good idea to combine railways and canals whenever possible in future paintings. This seemed a very good idea, so we decided that I would make a start with a painting of the scene we had just found.

Canals opened up a whole new area of research, so shortly afterwards I paid a visit to the National Waterways Museum at Stoke Bruerne, not far from Northampton, to see what was available by way of reference material. In the museum I found a full-size model of the cabin of a boat called *Sunny Valley*, in the colours of the Samuel Barlow Coal Co. This was perfect for the painting I had in mind, so I photographed all the details of the livery, bought a few reference books and set to work to learn something of the world of narrow boats.

Preliminary research revealed *Sunny Valley* to be quite a famous boat, having been used for a publicity film during the war years. Although it was a 'butty', which would normally have been towed by a motor boat, it had been fitted with an engine for the filming. This was later removed and the boat resumed its normal duties. The original boat is now preserved as it appears in the painting.

I decided to make the train a 'double-header', with one of the then almost new Hawksworth 'Counties' as the leading engine. Coming from Northampton, there could be only one choice, so No 1022 *County of Northampton* duly appeared in the painting.

The village provided some difficulties. The large barn in the middle distance is now a stylish barn conversion and the site of the cowsheds is now occupied by bungalows. All of these had to be somehow returned to their former appearance, so I needed some photographs of the village from roughly the right period. I decided that the best place to start would be the village pub, and was rewarded by a mine of information about the village. One of the residents had a photograph taken from the station footbridge in the early 1950s, which showed all the buildings I needed, and it was this one picture that made the painting possible.

The view from the footbridge at Lower Heyford, on the Banbury to London main line via Oxford.

'The Summer of '47'
30in x 20in

# 'THE ZULU'

The Great Western broad gauge finally disappeared in May 1892, which makes this the 'oldest' picture I have ever been asked to paint. Some years ago now I was contacted by a gentleman, unfortunately now deceased but then living near Bristol, who had seen a picture I had painted for a friend of his. He had decided that he would like one for himself and came up with the most unusual request. His grandfather had been the station master at Worle Junction during the transition from broad to standard gauge in the early 1890s. He had in his possession a book containing a photograph, taken in 1891 by the Rev A. H. Malan, in which his grandfather actually appeared, and asked me if I could adapt it into a painting. With some trepidation I arranged to meet him to see what could be done, thinking that perhaps this was a little too far in the past to be a feasible proposition. To my amazement, the photograph was of remarkably good quality and showed a moving train, hauled by one of Sir Daniel Gooch's 'Rover' Class locomotives. Worle Junction station, just off the main line on the Weston-super-Mare loop, was just discernible in the background. The train was some distance away as, at the time, it wasn't possible to stop movement satisfactorily with the photographic equipment available.

After some discussion, we decided that by moving the train forward and researching Worle Junction station for more detail, something might be done. The locomotive didn't pose much of a problem as the 'Rovers' are quite well documented, considering their age. They were magnificent machines of massive proportions, the top of the chimney standing 14ft 4in above rail level, and before long I was quite looking forward to putting one into a painting. The engines were always known only by their names and were never numbered; the one my client wanted was *Inkermann*. This was actually the second locomotive to carry the name, the first having been scrapped in the 1870s and replaced by a locomotive of virtually identical design.

Just before the change to standard gauge, the Great Western passenger rolling stock was a marvellous conglomeration of varied designs. Some coaches were convertible, having standard gauge bodies on broad gauge underframes; others were still to the full broad gauge dimensions. My library eventually produced one or two clear photographs of broad gauge convertible coaches, so I put these at the front of the train as I had a better idea of what they looked like. The true broad gauge coaches towards the rear of the train came from a postcard published soon after 1900 by the Locomotive Publishing Co. Worle Junction station proved surprisingly easy, one reference providing details of the station buildings, the platform shelter and even a couple of signals.

The 'Zulu' was an unofficial title given to the 11.15am express from Penzance to Paddington. The name began to be used during the summer of 1879 and is thought to be a reference to the Zulu War, which was being widely reported in the newspapers at the time.

'THE ZULU'
24in x 18in

# 'TWO WEEKS IN A WELSH TOWN'

**D**eganwy is a large village cum small town spread out along the Conwy estuary between Llandudno Junction and Llandudno Town. In common with many other places in the area, it is very picturesque and a client was very keen to have a painting recording his memories of numerous summer holidays he and his family had spent there. He had his own photographs, taken over a period of several years, all of which showed diesels or multiple units, but he wanted his painting to feature a steam train. The painting was to be set well into the period following the end of steam on British Railways, which meant that it had to feature the preservation era. The locomotive he wanted was a Stanier Class 5.

The location visit coincided with one of my clients' holidays in Deganwy, so we met on the station to look for a suitable spot for the painting. Deganwy station is right up against the sea wall, making it quite difficult to include the main street as well as the estuary. My client had several photographs taken from the signal box, which stands at the end of the down platform and has a commanding view of the main street, the station buildings, the beach and the hills beyond. We decided that this was the view to go for and it is the one now featured in the painting.

A close study of his photographs revealed some amusing details. In every one, taken over a period of several years, a Land Rover appeared in the same spot in the station car park. In later views it had been fitted with a new door, painted in a different colour from the rest of the vehicle. The telephone box changed from the familiar red variety to a more modern glass example and some of the shops along the main street were redecorated. The painting later appeared in a guild exhibition in Kidderminster, where I met a friend of a friend who actually lived in Deganwy. He was able to date the painting almost exactly as he knew when the red telephone box was changed. It just goes to show that thorough research pays dividends.

The engine we chose was No 45110, which at the time was often to be found on steam specials in various parts of the country. I remember one memorable excursion when it took a 14-coach train up the bank out of Holyhead by itself. As the train got slower and slower, bets were being laid as to whether it would make it to the top. In the event, it passed the summit at about 4mph!

For the weather, I chose the conditions I remembered from my own holidays in the area. Unpredictable weather seemed to be an occupational hazard along the North Wales coast and showers were to be expected at least several times during two weeks in a Welsh town.

'Two weeks in a Welsh Town'
36in x 24in

# 'WESTERN WORKHORSE'

A telephone call from a client who already owned one of my paintings set in motion what appeared at first sight to be a perfectly straightforward commission. He had managed to collect the smokebox numberplate, the cab-side numberplate and a nameplate from Great Western 'Hall' Class No 4999 *Gopsal Hall*, and he wanted the locomotive portrayed with a suitable signal box and some typical signals. He insisted, however, that it had to be the left-hand side of the engine. When I asked him why, he said that it was because he had the left-hand nameplate. I had no idea that they were any different, until he told me that it was stamped on the back 'LH'. After some research, I decided on Whiteball signal box, on the Somerset/Devon border, which seemed to me to typify a rural Great Western scene. He also wanted the engine to be green, which at first didn't seem to be a problem.

Most of the photographs available showed a rather ordinary-looking signal box that my client wasn't keen on, preferring the original and more picturesque Bristol & Exeter design. The 'Hall' Class, being mixed-traffic engines, had been painted black following nationalisation and it wasn't until midway through 1955 that they began to appear again in green livery, so this governed the period during which the painting had to be set. From this point, the research became more and more complicated. At around August 1955 the track layout was changed and two courses of stonework were added to the top of the wall on the right of the picture. Shortly after this, in November 1955, one of the signalmen upset an oil lamp in the signal box. The resulting fire destroyed the box down to the level of the stonework, after which it was rebuilt in a more modern and much less interesting design.

I then set about finding photographs of the original signal box, but only managed to discover one of the eastern side, which was dated as long ago as 1912. It was during a telephone conversation with Dick Riley, the eminent railway photographer, that the reason for this became apparent. He told me, 'When you had hefted a press camera, a quantity of glass plates and a heavy bag full of equipment up the line from Burlescombe station, about a mile away, you tended to be reluctant to waste exposures on subjects against the light, which made a decent result improbable.' In the end I decided to guess what the eastern side of the signal box might have looked like, while assuring my client that if it turned out to be different, I'd take the painting back and alter it. He seemed quite happy with this, so the painting was duly finished and delivered.

About 18 months later, during a visit to the West Somerset Railway, I met a gentleman from Taunton, Bert Chaffey ISM. He had a friend who had once worked on the banking engines from Wellington to Whiteball. He offered to show his friend a print of the painting in the hope that he might confirm what I had guessed regarding the appearance of the eastern side of the signal box. Not long afterwards I got a phone call from Bert, who said that his friend had confirmed that, in his opinion, the signal box was exactly right and 'he would have liked as many pounds as the number of times he'd been up those steps'. It was with a great sense of relief that I telephoned the owner to tell him that the painting was correct and didn't need altering. So, here we have No 4999 *Gopsal Hall* passing the original Whiteball signal box in September 1955 with an eastbound parcels train from Exeter to Bristol. As to whether the signalman watching the train is actually the one who later burned it down, your guess is as good as mine.

'WESTERN WORKHOUSE'
24in x 18in

# 'WINTER WAYFARERS'

The idea for this painting came from my wife, who thought that a snow scene with some narrow boats would make an attractive picture. She was right as usual, and the painting eventually became a very popular print. At the time, however, I was busy with a lot of other work, so it was a year or two before it was possible to make a start on the picture. As a preliminary, we got to work with a map and identified several possible locations on the Grand Union and Oxford canals not too far from home. We made visits to all those on the Grand Union only to find that none was suitable, mainly due to the distance between the railway and the canal. Some more searching turned up Stretton-under-Fosse, between Rugby and Nuneaton, on the Oxford Canal. This location proved to be perfect, with the railway and canal running side-by-side for about a mile and only a few yards apart. It is still possible to visit the spot, but from the towpath the railway is now almost completely masked by trees. Luckily, it was quite a popular spot for

The Oxford Canal at Stretton-under-Fosse with the West Coast Main Line running alongside, providing the location for 'Winter Wayfarers'.

photography in LMS days, so it was easy to find references of how it appeared during the late 1930s, when the picture is set.

Some research at the National Waterways Museum revealed that Fellows, Morton & Clayton Ltd had a large fleet of boats that were well known on the canals throughout the Midlands, so I decided to include a pair of their boats in the painting. For the train I chose the 'Coronation Scot', in its blue and silver livery of the late 1930s. I only ever saw one streamlined 'Coronation', a very tired, black and dishevelled *City of Lancaster*, just before its casing was removed in 1949. To restore one to its former glory would, I thought, suit a winter scene very well. To complete the composition, I included our friend Charles, taking his dog Sam for a walk along the towpath.

All went well, the picture was finished and I gave it to Mary, whose idea it had been in the first place. Not long afterwards, during a visit to the West Somerset Railway, I met Colin Marsden, who at the time was working for *The Railway Magazine*. He had seen a postcard of the painting and suggested that I should send it to Peter Kelly, then the editor of the magazine. Shortly afterwards it appeared as a centre spread in the magazine, and within half an hour we had two telephone calls asking about its availability for purchase. The first was from a very famous railway enthusiast and pop impresario whose name, I hate to admit, meant nothing to me at the time. The location is only a few miles from Coventry, his home town, and he had been taken fishing there many times as a small boy. I told him that the picture belonged to my manager and he then spent the next 15 minutes trying to persuade her to sell it to him. In the end he succeeded and we arranged that he would collect it. I'm not sure whether anyone thought to tell him its size, but he arrived in a fairly small sports hatchback. To get the picture, which measured almost 4 feet by 3 feet, into the car, we had to thread it through the rear window. It filled the rear of the car almost to capacity and left very little space for his passenger. So, after only a few weeks, Mary's ownership of the painting came to an abrupt end, but 'it's an ill wind', and the proceeds helped towards a superb holiday in India and Nepal soon afterwards!

'Winter Wayfarers'
36in x 24in

# LIST OF PLATES